Introduction

These days a seemingly endless number of TV channels assault a viewer's senses, channels covering everything from vintage films to news, sport to documentaries, history to what's happening right now, and it's all on tap 24 hours a day, 365 days a year.

It's a far cry from the days when, in the UK at least, there were but two programme providers – BBC and ITV – neither of which hosted much for the motorcycle-mad youngsters like me in their Saturday afternoon sports programmes. Yes, there were the televised scrambles, even trials at one point and the road racers got a boost when Barry Sheene grabbed the media's attention, but compared with other sports it was pretty much small potatoes.

Yet there was a motorcycle sport almost tailor-made for TV viewing. It was fast, it was furious… four riders, four laps. It seemed to last for four seconds then the next four were on the line in an endless stream of flat-out action with no boring bits. These riders on minimal motorcycles – little more than a frame, engine and a wheel at either end – revved their machines to the max until the start tapes went up. Then, in a crescendo of noise, flung their machines sideways into turns, sliding, slipping, drifting, passing, re-passing, and yes occasionally crashing in the jaw-dropping spectacle that was speedway!

Team colours for home matches, national colours for the big international finals, crowds of 70, 80 and 90,000 were not uncommon.

Names such as Olsen, Michanek, Collins, Boocock, Mauger and Briggs flashed past on the screen as they hurled flimsy-looking 500cc machines around a quarter-mile oval, dicing for the lead on the straights, flinging themselves sideways in the turns, throwing up plumes of dirt in what seemed to be barely controlled mayhem. But it wasn't mayhem, with riders simply going flat out and hanging on. No, there was much more to it than that. There was precise throttle control, balance and poise as the good riders vied for position, and as riders touched the tapes cheers from the crowds went up as favourites won, and groans reverberated when they didn't.

This bookazine is our take on that glorious spectacle of floodlit racing, bringing you the sound, the smell and the shale of speedway in its pre-laydown golden era.

Tim Britton

Contents

Some pictures just define a sport and this one of Ivan Mauger just about to throw it sideways could epitomise the whole speedway scene. Ivan of course is the 'winningest' racer in this whole scene and to celebrate one of his world championships, friends gold-plated his 500cc Jawa.

ON THE COVER

Speedway's golden boy Ivan Mauger, caught in action by Nick Nicholls in the Seventies, forms our main cover picture – with a line-up featuring Rudge's speedway machine from 1929, then Peter Collins on his way to his world title in 1976 and finally a mid-Fifties Rotrax typifying what was being raced in the period.

PROFILED

Take a series of superb machines, do some detail shots and a pic of either side, write some words based on the bike's background and hey presto, our 'profiled' series.

FEATURES

CLASSIC ACTION

Seeking out pics for this publication, we found oddball stuff which didn't fit into the chapters – so 'Classic Action' it is.

The man with the golden bike: New Zealander Ivan Mauger in action.

EDITOR AND AUTHOR: Tim Britton

PRODUCTION EDITORS:
Jack Harrison, Pauline Hawkins

DESIGN:
Chris Stringer, atg-media.com

COVER DESIGN:
Michael Baumber

ADVERTISING MANAGER:
Susan Keily

REPROGRAPHICS:
Jonathan Schofield
and Paul Fincham

PUBLISHER: Steve O'Hara

PUBLISHING DIRECTOR:
Dan Savage

**COMMERCIAL
DIRECTOR:**
Nigel Hole

**MARKETING
MANAGER:**
Charlotte Park
cpark@mortons.co.uk

DISTRIBUTION:
tradesales@mortons.co.uk
classicmagazines.co.uk/
tradesales

PRINTED BY:
William Gibbons And Sons,
Wolverhampton

ISBN: 978-1-911276-00-5

PUBLISHED BY:
Mortons Media Group Ltd, Media Centre,
Morton Way, Horncastle, Lincolnshire
LN9 6JR
Tel: 01507 529529

COPYRIGHT
Mortons Media Group Ltd, 2017
All rights reserved.

A FAMILY AFFAIR

Admitting to being attracted to speedway by watching his older brother Nigel racing, Eric Boocock quickly made his mark on the sport and – as in the meeting where this picture was taken – both Booeys teamed up for pairs races. The occasion is an international against Sweden in July 1972 where Eric Boocock helped England dominate to beat the visitors 35 points to 29. Despite a valiant effort by the Swedes the Boocock phenomenon forged ahead and created an eight-point gap in the overall championship that the Scandinavians couldn't close.

Noted for a tidy style Eric is right at the top of his game here and regularly placed on the podium of the British championships which he would win in 1974. After his career as a racer Eric put a lot back into the sport in his role as team manager, and Peter Collins cites Booey's help and guidance as a major part of his world championship win. Eric is still involved in the sport and remains as enthusiastic about it as ever.

IN AT THE START

One of the earliest major venues – if not the very first – for the exciting new dirt track/speedway sensation in the UK was Stamford Bridge, the home of Chelsea Football Club capitalising quickly on the popularity of the new sport by hosting a race on May 5, 1928. The sport rivalled football in the entertainment stakes, and that's certainly in evidence in this shot taken in 1929. Unfortunately, speedway was short-lived at the stadium when its team – known as The Pensioners and captained by Gus Kuhn – folded in 1932. It's a great shame, as they were one of the pioneers of speedway racing having claimed victory in the 1929 Southern League Championship.

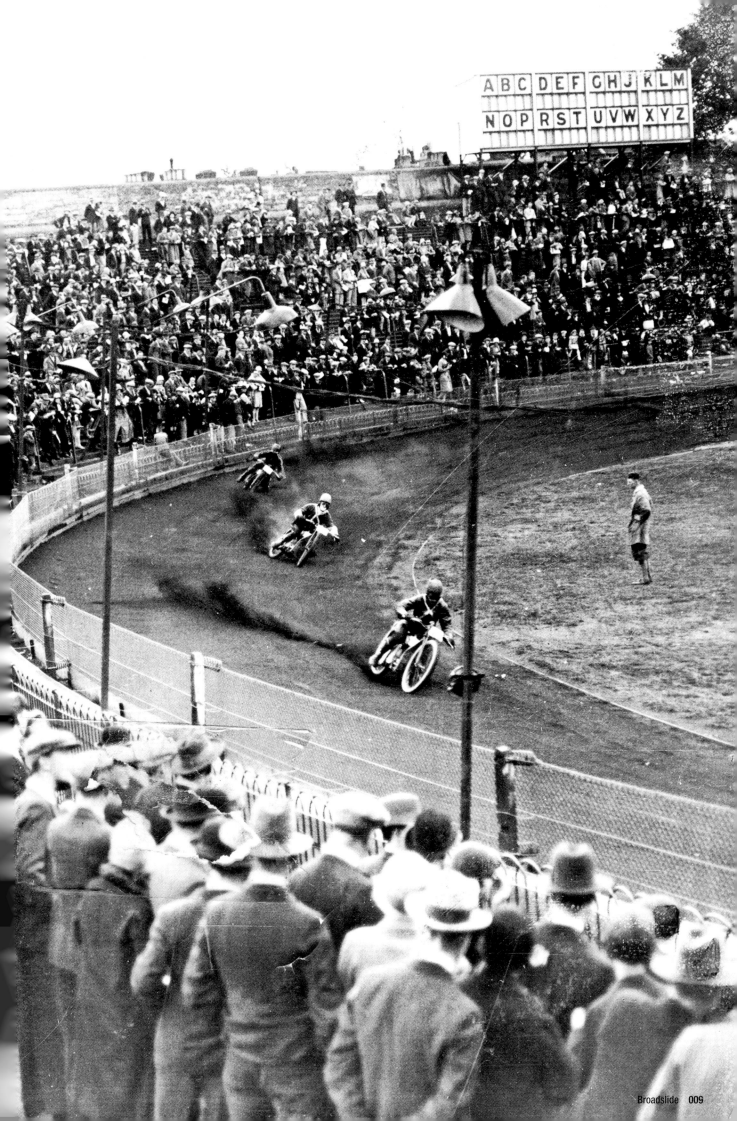

1928 Rudge

Rudge was one of the manufacturers that tapped into the speedway
market early on, and was able to provide what riders wanted quite quickly.

TOP LEFT CLOCKWISE: Though the magneto is vulnerable in the front position, a deflector plate shields it. Short race duration and alcohol fuels keep temperatures down.

Four valves? In 1928? Oh yes! Some 50 years later these were the 'new thing' – note plug position is now central. Rockers get a pump of grease as lube.

Minimal suspension is all that's required at the front, just enough to smooth out the bumps. Rudge's spring box does the job.

Not a difficult thing to make and has the benefits of being protected, easily mounted and light. Capacity isn't a problem thanks to short races.

As this new-to-the-UK sport of sliding motorcycles around a dirt track started to take hold of the public's imagination, it woke manufacturers up to potential sales. Or, more accurately, woke them up to the fact they were missing potential sales. Some caught on quicker than others, and one of those companies that realised Douglas was having it all its own way in 1928 was Rudge. In very short order, Rudge had what is probably the world's first purpose-built speedway bike that was available for the racers of the day to buy.

This particular one is from the Colin Knight collection and is near enough as he bought it, as he explained during the photoshoot. It even runs well enough for former world champion Billy Hamill to have ridden it recently at Rye House Speedway during a Men in Black demo.

Everything except the Dunlop wheel rims, magneto and Amal single-float carburettor were made by Rudge. The bike sports plenty of items that became standard in speedway such as lightweight hubs, a remote oil tank, tiny, underslung fuel tank, single-cylinder engine, big rear sprocket and countershaft gearbox to hang the Rudge eight-spring clutch on.

Rudge did rely quite heavily on traditional ▶

LEFT: Knock-on and knock-off facility means gearing changes can happen as fast as possible so the bike is always geared for the conditions on an ever-changing track.

BELOW: Comfort isn't high on the list of priorities for a racer…

RIGHT: Rudge's four-valve engine was quite advanced for its day.

Colin Knight was asked to pose with his favourite bike from the collection. He chose the Rudge.

ABOVE: As long as there's enough oil in for the race, why carry any more? The carburettor is jetted for methanol and there's no filter fitted…

ABOVE: The front forks are Rudge's own girder type, stiff enough for speedway. The minimal guard stops a little dirt from flying up.

There's nothing on the bike that doesn't do a job. A speedway track is no place for fripperies; it's out, race and in.

ABOVE: The primary drive is simple and wears a cover for safety reasons. Keeping the clutch clean and adjusted is a major part of the maintenance routine.

The footrest is basic, but strong enough for a four-lap race.

LEFT: The exhaust pipes are just long enough for power, the dirt shield protects the exposed valve springs and no cover means heat can escape from the top of the engine.

methods of construction for the speedway bike and so the frame is made up of cast-iron lugs with tube brazed in. Rumour has it this type of construction resists the vibration from single-cylinder engines better, though it is a heavier method. Rudge's choice of engine must have also raised eyebrows a little in the late 1920s; the four-valve configuration on a single was not unknown but certainly not commonplace. Colin says the engine is probably a special 'works' one as it differs slightly from production units which would have the spark plug angled at the side, whereas this particular engine has the plug mounted centrally where it's shielded from the airflow by the rockers and valves. This isn't so much a problem as, even with a cast-iron engine, heat dissipation is excellent when dope fuel is used.

Given the short duration of speedway races, this motor has no need of a recirculating oil pump – instead relying on total-loss splash lubrication with a manually adjustable flow rate. The castor oil is fed from a remote tank, does its lube duties and drains into the sump where a plug can be removed between races to drain what's been collected. Nor does the gearbox require any gear cluster, and inside is only a countershaft and Castrol R for lubrication.

Belle Vue Speedway

40 YEARS OF

1928·1968

SPEEDWAY

Saturday, April 6th, 1968. 1210th Meeting

CHALLENGE MATCH

BELLE VUE

v.

SHEFFIELD

9D

Held under the Regulations of the Speedway Control Board

Chapter 1

History

Originating in Australia as a carnival attraction, it wouldn't take long for no-frills dirt track racing to catch on and become the first incarnation of what we know today as speedway...

Speedway was a relative latecomer to the sporting scene. Unlike trials riding where the MCC was running long-distance events in the veteran era, or even the TT which was launched on the sporting world in 1907, it was the end of the 1920s before the spectacle took hold in the UK.

It is possible to argue the case for all racing before the adoption of Tarmac or concrete road surfaces as being 'dirt track', and certainly pre-First World War American motorcyclists were using oval circuits – of the horse-racing trotting track type – to race their motorcycles on. These ovals were much safer than the board tracks built in other parts of the USA; tracks made from a million linear feet of timber and having steep banking at either end – 30 degrees initially, but as steep as 60 degrees towards the end of their time. Phenomenal speeds were attained

with 100mph commonplace pre-1910, but it meant accidents were just as regular, and such was the public outcry that the safer option of a dirt circuit was opted for.

From such early beginnings emerged Class C flat track racing, which has few similarities to speedway. Generally added to a county fair, this dirt track racing was seen as an attraction rather than a sport; and it was this concept that prompted a lad called John S Hoskins to add extra value to the 1923 West Maitland Grand Electric Light Carnival Weekend.

A general consensus is that the very first 'speedway' meeting in the UK took place at High Beech, Epping Forest on February 19, 1928, though there is a case to be put for a Camberley meeting some 10 months earlier in May 1927 as being the first dirt track tournament in the country. There is little doubt, however, that both meetings were inspired

by the efforts of Johnnie Hoskins, a New Zealander who was a promoter at the West Maitland Horse Trotting Track in New South Wales, Australia. A motorcycle enthusiast, Hoskins – in a stroke of genius which credits him as the inventor of speedway – was looking for extra attractions for his event and invited local motorcyclists to remove the lights and mudguards from their machines and race round the track for a first prize of £10.

The trotting track was an oval. Horses raced anti-clockwise so all carnival attendees easily understood the concept of the motorcycle race, and by all accounts it proved hugely popular on the day. For some reason one of the few rules or regulations for the meeting was a requirement for riders to keep their feet on the footrests at all times. Once riders discovered the fastest way around the track was to broadside a ▶

There is dispute over what can actually be classed as the first speedway race in the UK. Camberley Heath in May 1927 staked its claim but the format was clockwise not anti-clockwise.

LEFT: In contrast, a meeting held at High Beech a few months after Camberley was much more like the speedway we know today.

machine while trailing their left leg in the cinders, this 'feet up' rule was ignored.

News of this exciting new spectacle spread rapidly and soon meetings were being staged on tracks in any number of Australian towns and cities, and it wasn't long before interest grew internationally. In the UK, Camberley MCC felt it knew what this odd sport from Australia was all about and with the assistance of the military laid out a track on Camberley Heath in early May 1927. A headline in *The Motor Cycle* of May 12, 1927, screamed 'Dirt Track Racing at Camberley' and proclaimed that dirt track had arrived in the UK following this successful, if novel, event. Unlike the Australian version though, Camberley had decided to run clockwise round the quarter-mile track consisting of two straights joined at either

end with a semi-circle to give a slightly flattened oval shape. It didn't deter the massive crowd who turned up to see this event and witness Mr C Harman and Miss Fay Taylour share the spoils on the day.

THE BIRTH OF MODERN-DAY SPEEDWAY

If the direction of the track seems odd to us the format was much more familiar with a series of four-lap heats, but with three riders per heat instead of four and the winners of each heat going through to the finals. Something else familiar to modern speedway enthusiasts is that there was a restart after Miss Taylour jumped the flag in the 350 final. During the restart all three riders left the line together, handlebar-to-handlebar, as they shot towards the first turn. Harman nosed his

OK-Supreme into the lead with Taylour's AJS on his rear wheel. The third man, Mr Martin on a Velocette, elected to remain in bottom gear for the whole race but retired after the second lap with gearbox troubles. Despite a valiant effort by Taylour it was Harman who won the 350 final. To prove it was no fluke he rode his 350 OK-Supreme in the 500 final and won that too, even rubbing it in by being left on the startline in neutral as the other two riders, Messrs Beard and Shearing roared off on their Sunbeam and Ariel respectively. Harman must have been a handy rider as 200 yards later he was in the lead.

Proving herself to be no slouch, Taylour dominated the unlimited class making up for being bested in the 350 final by leading from start to finish. Taylour took the flag 20 yards ahead of Harman whose smoking clutch showed how hard he'd been trying to keep the revs up. Sidecar enthusiasts were not forgotten and there were four brave/mad (delete as appropriate) crews showing they too could drift with the best. In the spirit of the day the solo winner Harman bolted a sidecar to his 350 OK-Supreme and did battle successfully against outfits three times the capacity of his. *The Motor Cycle* recorded Harman's

JOHNNIE HOSKINS MBE: THE FATHER OF SPEEDWAY

As far as we know New Zealand doesn't have the monopoly on characters at the top of the speedway tree, but it does sometimes seem that way. Johnnie was one such character, and he's credited with the invention of the sport when looking for an attraction to add to his displays at West Maitland trotting track in Australia.

Arriving in England in 1928, aboard the SS *Oronsay* – a ship he once referred to as the *Mayflower* of speedway in later life – with 20 riders he quickly established a scene in the UK.

By 1930 there were 70 tracks operating, most with some involvement from Hoskins. When the speedway leagues were formed, Hoskins again was at the forefront of promotion being involved at Newcastle, Edinburgh, Glasgow, West Ham, Bradford and Belle Vue. He was chairman of the second division, president of the national league and in 1977 was presented with the Grand Master of Speedway medal at Belle Vue.

In 1979 the UK recognised Johnnie's achievements and he was made an MBE at Buckingham Palace – presented by Charles, Prince of Wales – where Hoskins admitted he had never been a speedway racer. A promoter to the last, Hoskins passed away peacefully in Kent in 1987 aged 94.

FAY TAYLOUR: SPEEDWAY GLAMOUR

Contemporary biographies of 'Flying' Fay Taylour portray a woman with a strong sense of competitive spirit and of a personality not easily daunted. From a relatively well-to-do background in Ireland, where she attended a prestigious ladies' college for education, Taylour won a monetary prize for domestic science and invested it in a Levis two-stroke motorcycle. That lasted for three days, before being replaced by a four-stroke Levis and then a 350 AJS.

With her retired army officer father living near Reading, Fay moved there and began competing in trials – a highlight was winning an ISDT silver medal – and the new sport of scrambling. Her appetite for competition meant Fay was naturally attracted to all motorcycle sport and was on hand to enter the Ilford Light Car and Motorcycle Club dirt track at Camberley in 1927. Against strong opposition Taylour did remarkably well and embarked on a speedway career when the sport finally arrived in the UK. Such was her skill she was invited to race in New Zealand and Australia against acknowledged experts. Much to their surprise the fiery redhead beat a considerable number of them, but to her dismay she found out on her return to the UK that women had been banned from racing speedway.

Needing an outlet for her competitive urge, Fay turned her hand to car racing and was equally successful on four wheels in the 1930s. Her political sympathies led to internment on the Isle of Man for part of the Second World War, but she was allowed to move to Ireland latterly. Postwar, Taylour sold British cars to Hollywood stars in the USA and was invited to attend New Cross Speedway's 20th anniversary in 1948. She tried, unsuccessfully, to have the ban lifted on female racers at that time so embarked on a Formula 500 car racing career, beating then current speedway ace Olle Nygren in Sweden. Taylour lived out her life in Dorset where a book she was writing about her life was curtailed by her death in 1983.

ABOVE: The safety run-off areas look a little basic as, even in those carefree days of low-powered machines, a faller could send his bike into the crowd.

ABOVE: With riders actually looking like they were racers rather than just a bunch of lads who turned up and made a bit of noise, the spectacle caught the public's eye.

attempts as fast and clean while the second-place man, Webb, was more spectacular but in sliding lost a lot of ground. All in all it was agreed the dirt track experiment was successful and a superb day's sport.

The press of the day kept on about dirt track in Australia and it was clearly a sport that was going to take off, just needing a catalyst to do so. This catalyst came in two parts, first was Hoskins who'd capitalised on his successes at Maitland and was promoting the new sport all over Australia. The second was a feature in *The Motor Cycle* by Nitor on February 2, 1928 entitled Thrills of the Dirt Track. Nitor presented a contingent of Australian racers, likely including Hoskins, in London with the idea of promoting their style of dirt track. In order to whet the appetite of readers, Nitor (which, by the way, was a catch-all pen name used by several staffers at the publication) described a typical Australian dirt track meeting and it seems pretty familiar to modern enthusiasts. Setting the scene, Nitor invited readers to imagine a floodlit cinder track of approximately a third of a mile with two straights joined by semi-circles at either end. Promptly at 8pm the first race begins; a flying mile with two racers who hurtle towards the first bend with flames spouting from their exhausts. A touch on the ignition cut-out

button kills the power for an instant then lets it back in at full throttle. The bike broadslides, each rider sending up sparks from steel-shod left boots, wheels churning up a plume of cinders. No time to look behind as the bars are wrenched straight and the rider flashes down the straight to hit the kill button again to throw the machine sideways at 60mph. Suddenly it all goes wrong for the leader, he steps off his machine and rolls, over and over at 60, 50, 40mph until he finally stops, picks himself up and checks to see how his mount has fared. This, claimed Nitor, is the sport that grasped the attention of Saturday night crowds in Brisbane, Adelaide, Sydney and many more places besides, knocking greyhound racing out of the court. A meeting has plenty of spills, lots of thrills and 20 races a night; this is what we wanted to see according to Nitor, and this is what happened at High Beech a few months after the Camberley meeting. Speedway had arrived.

idecars were part of the fledgling sport, but the 'barrow lads'
oon realised that going the other way round was much better.

GET YOUR KNEE DOWN SON

Way back in the early days of this exciting new sport, the fast way round the corner was for a rider to trail his leg to the rear of the bike and get his knee down while leaning over at an incredible angle. The caption on the back of the print from which this image is taken simply reads: "vintage leg trailing demonstration by dirt track Douglas rider took place during the interval." Even though it's a slightly fuzzy reproduction, the sheer exuberance of the rider shines through and for that reason alone the image makes the cut. Enthusiasts will know the fore and aft Douglas twin was a popular machine in early racing during the 1920s, and could well be classed as a 'lay-down' engine bike.

Chapter 2

The early years

With all the hoo-ha there was a feeling this new-fangled type of racing could just be press hype, but it wasn't just Nitor bulling it up – this was the action the public wanted to see...

The popularity of dirt track racing soon caught on, and before long thousands were flocking to meetings.

Some 20,000 or more spectators made their way by car, motorcycle, bicycle, bus and on foot to High Beech – or more accurately Kings Oak Speedway, Loughton, Essex – a fortnight after Nitor's February 1928 article appeared in *The Motor Cycle* for what would become the very first proper speedway meet in the UK.

Set on the perimeter of a sports track and organised by Ilford Light Car and Motorcycle Club, a track comprising roughly a square with rounded corners and a surface made of cinders rather than dirt had been laid out. This made it quite a firm surface to race on and until competitors had a chance to try it in heats there were few broadslides. Once the riders got the gist of the track the thrills began and with heats of five laps and races of three laps with three riders in each, the pace was kept up throughout the day from the 10.30am start to the 5pm finish.

Big bikes, small bikes, solos and sidecars, novices and experienced racers all battled it out in this newest of sports.

While it was true there lacked a certain atmosphere afforded to those familiar with speedway's floodlit night meets in Australia, there was plenty of action. There were upsets, too, such as Mr LP Wilson on a 172 Villiers-engined Francis-Barnett challenging the 500cc four-strokes and almost beating a few. His efforts eliciting the comment from a reporter: "One more pony in the engine and he would have won."

As the day wore on riders became more daring and the narrow squeaks, tussles and spills became more frequent. Proof, if proof were needed, of the competitive nature of the riders came in the seventh heat. With the reporter for *The Motor Cycle* describing the heat, three riders lined up for the start; Messrs Medcalf and Harley rocketed away from the

ABOVE: There was a thriving sidecar industry in the UK at the time, and owners and enthusiasts expected to see the three-wheelers in action.

line but Mr Barrett on his P and P was left behind. Not to be outdone by the faster pair he forced his way past Harley and challenged the leader – handlebar-to-handlebar – as they hurtled round the track until, almost inevitably, their "bars touched and both riders looped the loop in an incident that brought screams from the ladies watching and gasps of horror from even the most staid of spectators". It seems in those far-off days the spills were regarded as part of the fun and neither rider was injured physically, although pride is a different matter.

The three-wheeled brigade wouldn't be left out of the fun, and the sidecars had their own heats and finals but with only two outfits in the race each time. There was a slight tweak to the running of the sidecar events as it was deemed a bit hairy for the two outfits to race together in the finals, so each heat winner had the course to themselves with the overall winner being decided on a fastest-time basis. At the end of the day – the crowds gone home, the racers departed, the circuit littered with rubbish – those who had witnessed this exciting spectacle had been left in no doubt they were on the verge of something really big. *The Motor Cycle* tended

to concur as its Items of Interest page detailed a forthcoming dirt track meeting to be held in March 1928 at the Audenshaw Trotting Track near Manchester. It was to be organised by the same people who arranged the Belle Vue TT, and the trotting lap record of 28mph was expected to be easily broken.

So, as the 1920s came to a close, the world had a new sport – one that would capture the imagination of motorcyclists and non-motorcyclists alike as clubs and tracks sprang up all over the UK. Such was the interest and confidence that it was something 'here to stay', 17 of the major motorcycle manufacturers of the time listed dirt track models in their catalogues for the Olympia Show in November 1928. On the lead-up to the show, the whole concept of dirt track racing and its organisation was the subject of several comprehensive articles from Nitor and the illustrious Ixion – the pen name of motorcycle journalist Canon Basil Hart Davies – both suggesting ways in which the sport could progress. Some ideas were adopted, some weren't, but either way the indisputable fact is that by the 1930s speedway had hit the big time.

BELOW: Mr Ed Lawrence was reported in the press as "giving an American touch to the first British Dirt Track" on his 500cc Ariel.

Chapter 3

What might have been

Both Greeves and BSA tried and failed to create a winning speedway machine, and research into the second of these efforts uncovered a gallery of never-before-seen photographs...

There had been any number of attempts to produce a motor suitable for the speedway scene, some successful – the Jawa/ESO, Weslake, GM to name three – and some that ought to have been successful but failed for various reasons – the BVR is one such example.

On the face of it there should be no reason why a speedway motor couldn't be produced quite easily, after all it's not exactly complicated being a single-cylinder unit. JAP had been dominating the sport with an engine designed in the 1930s and updated by development rather than radically changing things, as a result these engines were still being used to great effect up to the 1960s.

There were newcomers to the market and with Barry Briggs's help the ESO unit would, under the Jawa name, come to dominate the world market in a very short space of time.

During research for this publication, many hours were spent trawling through the archives at Mortons Media Group, the company holding the back issues and rights to *Motor Cycling* and *The Motor Cycle* which, under their nicknames Green 'Un and Blue 'Un – derived from the colour of their masthead backgrounds – were the premier motorcycling publications in the world in their time. These weekly magazines covered every aspect of

motorcycling and thanks to their longevity – *The Motor Cycle* was started in 1902 while *Motor Cycling* came along a little later in 1911 – were seen as part of the industry. Even in the 1960s, when their slightly home counties' style of writing was becoming outdated for the motorcycle-buying youngster, they could still be relied upon to pitch up with interesting features and two that leapt out for me were ideal for *Broadslide*.

Both articles were based around respected makers, one of which had produced a speedway machine in the first flush of the sport during the 20s and 30s, attempting to create a new engine. Neither would come to fruition.

ABOVE: The main purpose of the test day was to put laps on the bike. There's mention of a hundred laps by each rider, but we can't confirm that.

Coventry speedway ace Nigel Boocock puts the BSA through its paces. It's likely Booey senior is in his trademark blue leathers.

ABOVE: An adjustable trail on the Greeves's headstock.

ABOVE: Straight tubes, plenty of bolts, damage fixed easily.

BELOW: The test session included an earlier engine which didn't have the finning cut away, but was more standard.

GREEVES HAS A GO

The traditional speedway motor had been a four-stroke single with a long stroke that produced lots of usable power, but there was no real reason for it being a four-stroke as in the very early days all sorts of engines were used; twins, singles, 350cc, 500cc and even 600cc capacities as well as two- and four-strokes. It was this latter method of firing that interested Greeves's works rider Don Smith in the early 60s.

Don was a true motorcycle enthusiast and pretty much successful at whatever discipline he tackled. While at Greeves for trials, scrambles and enduro he also raced speedway for Hackney Wick near his own shop. He would also take on challenges others possibly would shy away from which is how *The Motor Cycle* was along at Hackney one afternoon while Bengt Jansson was screaming round the track on a two-stroke. After several impressive laps the Swede came in and announced: "This bike could revolutionise speedway!" Not that the bike was perfect; there were a few issues with the concept – it was a little down on power for starters – and out of the corners Jansson also felt the front forks were a little stiff. That said, he liked the 165lb flyweight machine and for a first-time running the Smith prototype was deemed successful.
The bike was giving away 140cc over the opposition but Smithy had a 390cc top end ready to bolt on, which was also tuned for methanol as a fuel rather than the petrol of the 360cc version.

Speaking to the reporter, Smithy said he'd got a few ideas to follow up on and the original frame – which was made from cheap tubing – would be remade in either Reynolds 531 or T45. Interestingly the frame was bolted up, and of mainly straight tubing.
The theory being damage would be easily and quickly correctable so the professional speedway racer would be back on track and earning; an important point for those lads who raced almost every night of the week.

He hinted his 390cc motor would have a one-and-a-quarter-inch choke, with a Wal Phillips fuel injector and reckoned the inlet tract could be an eighth bigger at the expense of bottom end power. He also added that if the tests proved successful (and to Don 'success' meant beating the JAP and ESO engines fair and square rather than expecting a two-stroke class to be launched) then his production machines would feature his own countershaft, magnesium hubs and a diaphragm clutch. It would be interesting to know what happened to this bike, as Don seemed keen to take it on to further things. Did the second prototype ever see light of day?

BSA ENTERS THE FRAY

It should, even as it struggled on in its death throes in 1973, have been relatively straightforward for the once-mighty BSA to produce a speedway machine. Big four-stroke singles were once the lifeblood of the company and there was still an industry behind them, plus Cyril Halliburn – responsible for the Gold Star single development – was in charge of the project. A bike was produced to see what BSA could achieve, and it was tested by Nigel Boocock and John Harrhy who were top lads in Coventry's speedway team. *The Motor Cycle* was invited along to this test at Brandon

ABOVE: This fellow's identity stumped us for a while as very little reference to him and his ability is in the records of this test day... recognise him yet? It's Rob North, frame wizard.

ABOVE: Had the project been taken up then Alistair Cave would have been responsible for putting it into production at BSA.

ABOVE: Cyril Halliburn was a factory man who did so much to make the BSA Gold Star into a reliable and powerful engine unit. He would be involved with the successor to the Goldie and may well have instigated this speedway test.

Stadium in late April 1973 where more than 100 laps were completed on the machine in front of technicians from Lucas and Amal.

The sorts of speeds and lap times being reached were up there with contemporary Jawa speeds and the assembled crowd was quietly confident with the test day. BSA works manager Al Cave was guarded in his comments though, saying the motor stood up well to the test day and the notes taken would provide useful information for a second prototype already under way.

Housed in a Rob

North speedway frame, the first test motor was based on a B50 motocross engine with its gearbox sawn off and mounting points built up with weld. The barrel was also off the B50 motocross machine, shortened a little to give a compression ratio suitable for use with methanol fuel.

However, after the test day a Mk 2 version of the engine was installed in the frame. This had crankcases cast from new patterns, a barrel with minimal finning and power of "between the JAP and Jawa". For the cylinder head a standard B50 casting was used, but altered radically to achieve the sort of power needed on a speedway track. In a shift from other speedway

engines, which use a total loss oil system, the BSA one has a dry sump with oil carried in the frame tubes and circulated with a low-output oil pump.

The ignition was provided by the then bang-up-to-the-minute Lucas Rita transistorised system which was reckoned to be no heavier than a magneto. In any case the whole bike had a claimed weight of a tad less than 180lb. The Cave/Halliburn team also said they were experimenting with various bore/stroke

BELOW: Power was supplied by a battery hung on the side, rather than an ignition system.

Cyril Halliburn is caught by the camera, Nigel Boocock strides purposefully across the track while Alistair Cave feigns disinterest.

ABOVE: This is a BSA B50 motor… but hold on, you say, the B50 was a unit engine with an integral gearbox? Yes it was, but with the aid of a hacksaw (BSA probably couldn't afford a milling machine at this point in the 70s) and some alloy welding gear, the B50 became a speedway unit.

BELOW: Some work on the finning to allow a greater air flow gave the BSA unit a distinctive look.

combinations plus port dimensions. They also told *The Motor Cycle* that BSA would have to find as big a market as possible for the engine in order for it to be viable, and they were looking at the grass- and sand-track market, but for now they were interested in proving the concept. Part of this proving would be trying the engine in actual race conditions, which would mean slipping it into some second-half races to see how it held up under the strain of racing rather than testing. Cave said: "Though there is still much to be done before production details can be finalised, we are happy with the results achieved so far."

With the benefit of 40 years of hindsight and the collapse of the industry, it has been reported that BSA was interested in knocking out one thousand units, dumping them on the market and walking away from the project. Not exactly the sort of back-up needed for those earning their living sliding round the speedway tracks of the world.

STOP THE PRESS!
In the search for material for this publication

all sorts of boxes in the archive have been turned upside down and emptied, with the contents viewed, dismissed, packed then reviewed. During such a session an innocent-looking package about 40mm wide and 150mm long dropped out. Such packages contain stripfilm and in the pre-digital days this was how images were stored. For younger readers who are more than likely familiar with the rapid turnaround of images available using phones, iPads and mini cameras, things were not always so. Generally a roll of film was fitted into an SLR and capable of taking 36 images in either positive or negative, and were sent away to be developed before anyone could see if the images were usable. Stored in small cases, these images could easily drop into the bottom of archive boxes as happened here.

The BSA speedway machine test was mentioned in the press of the day but no one I spoke to could recall any photographs of the day other than the few used in one weekly edition of *The Motor Cycle*.

Surely they must be somewhere, went the thinking, and the appropriate BSA box was

searched again – this time by taking stuff out rather than flicking through the sub folders. In desperation the rest of the BSA boxes (BSA occupies a decent space in the archive) were searched, and tucked away under everything else was the file with images taken on the day and yes, people did really wear such clothes and have such hairstyles. Even more remarkably, these are quite possibly the rarest BSA images ever.

There are several famous names clearly pictured. Nigel Boocock, of course, although it's a shame we couldn't show his blue leathers as in those days most images were black and white. Still, the shots show 'Booey the elder' blasting the prototype round a speedway track seemingly devoid of any impact points on the fence. Also pictured is a very young-looking Rob North who was certainly one of the better-known frame makers of the 70s. BSA chiefs Al Cave and Cyril Halliburn were there also, as was Booey's team-mate John Harrhy. Presumably other people in various pictures are Lucas and Amal technicians.

The newly discovered images are featured in this chapter.

ABOVE: Rob North discusses frames with Booey while John Harrhy seems amused.

Once out on track an expert like Nigel Boocock could really make the bike shift.

Here is 'Booey the elder' with a bit of lean on.

t's likely the BSA hierarchy would have wanted to make a thousand units, flog 'em and forget 'em.

Jap 'Long Five'

Though the frame looks like a Rotrax it isn't, and so many people copied the
Rotrax frame the company stopped making them. This could be a Duggan.

TOP LEFT CLOCKWISE: The JAP four-stud engine was fitted on the bike when it was purchased, but Colin tracked down the correct and more desirable five-stud race engine.

Oil for lubrication is carried in this small tank at the rear of the machine. Traditionally speedway bikes use castor-based oil and Rock Oil's version is in this tank.

The front wheel is spindly looking, probably because of the narrow, large-diameter tyres.

Later rear wheels are reversible, so when the tyre wears during a meeting it is an easy job to turn it so the sharp edge is presented to the track for grip.

There are many reasons for starting a collection of anything, but by far the most common where motorcycles are concerned is that famous line – 'I wanted one years ago'. Speedway super-enthusiast Colin Knight reckons he had no real intention of starting a collection, but always wanted a proper speedway JAP in the shed. "It matches what I used to watch being raced at West Ham, which inspired me to have a try at speedway," he said. Sadly it didn't go well for the young Mr Knight, and a badly broken leg convinced him that maybe restoring the bikes would be better than throwing them round a track.

This particular bike, with its chrome-plated frame, is reminiscent of the Rotrax frames which were popular with racers of the time because of the easy care and clean lines. The Rotrax Cycle Company was a Southampton-based maker of cycle frames for racing and competition that moved into speedway production when workshop foreman Mike Compton designed and built one for the sport. Like many good ideas it was copied, a lot. So, this frame isn't actually a Rotrax example, but one possibly made by Aussie racer Vic Duggan – a Haringay team man. As such the bike is typical of what the spectator would see on the track at each ▶

LEFT: There's minimal guarding on this bike.

BELOW: Dope motors sup fuel at a fantastic rate when flat out; twin taps need to be open during a race.

BELOW RIGHT: Letting a fuel pipe rest on a hot engine isn't a great idea. Some twists of copper wire dissipate heat, and all is well.

A threaded adjuster makes sure the wheel stays in place.

ABOVE: A Norton three-speed clutch stands up to the rigours of speedway quite well.

ABOVE: Twin-float carburettors make sure there is always enough fuel on hand for the engine to perform well.

Pretty much typical of the bikes Colin Knight was captivated by when they were racing at West Ham.

ABOVE: A double-feed oil pump is connected to the end of the cam wheel and driven by a slotted thimble. Lube it total-loss.

Tape is lighter than a grip and doesn't come loose. The ball-ended lever is a modern modification.

LEFT: A Rotrax countershaft was a popular fitment for speedway bikes.

meeting from the 1940s up to the late 1960s, and maybe later for the second-half riders.

Colin acquired the bike in one piece, but it came with a four-stud JAP motor instead of the desirable five-stud version. Luckily, Colin was able to locate a five-stud motor and the bike is as it should be – with a 15:1 compression ratio which on dope fuel churns out a usable 45bhp. Of course it needs a fair bit of fuel at that ratio so the Type 27 twin-float Amal was developed specifically for such use. The tank holds just enough dope for a speedway race, plus a little for safety. Typically, JAP used a Pilgrim oil pump and a total-loss lube system with castor-based Rock Oil in the remote tank.

All this power is fed through a Rotrax countershaft box and a Norton three-spring clutch which was used because of availability and strength. The job of putting all this power to use on the track was handled by a 22-inch rear wheel – the change to a smaller, 19-inch rear came in the 1960s. Like most of the frames by this period, the steering heads were bushed instead of having bearings to take the fork stem, in this case Rotrax – or possibly Duggan – forks which hold a 23-inch front wheel. Both the wheels wear Barum speedway tyres, but unlike later rear wheels this one isn't reversible.

Chapter 4

Briggo: The legend

Born in New Zealand, formed in the UK, Barry Briggs MBE has packed more into 82 years than anyone should be able to manage. To cram all he's done into a few pages is an impossible task; his own biography, Wembley and Beyond: My Incredible Journey, runs to nearly 500 pages. Tim Britton sat down with the man himself to get just a flavour of his incredible life and times...

Sitting talking to Barry Briggs during one of his visits to the UK was an experience not to be missed, and very early on in the several hours spent with him – as his other half Jan kept coffee, sandwiches and biscuits flowing – I formed the opinion that if ever a sportsperson should have his life made into a film it should be Briggo. Born on December 30, 1934, as the eldest of three brothers, Barry's early life was lived in a suburb of Christchurch in New Zealand until his parents' marital break-up in the 1940s forced a move to less well-to-do accommodation where young Briggo played a leading role in the welfare of his brothers Murray and Wayne... whether they wanted it or not.

He played a variety of sports before the thought of hurtling round a track on a motorcycle dawned on him. Rugby, football, boxing, hockey and wrestling all provided an outlet for his competitive nature. That competitiveness, which would ultimately propel him to the top of the unforgiving motorsport of speedway, found a new outlet on the cycle speedway tracks of New Zealand where a local hotshot called Ronnie Moore was showing the local lads the way round.

Cycle speedway was big at that time, maybe still is, and there was a hotbed of competition with numerous teams locked in two-wheeled combat at tracks laid out wherever they could. Naturally Briggo had his own methods of training for such racing and it involved being towed behind his cousin's Matchless. Once up to the required speed he would attempt to broadslide the bicycle but, quite understandably, the bicycle didn't always stand up to such treatment and by his own admission his mechanical skills were acquired by trial and error.

Briggo also recounted how he progressed to motorised transport by earning a bit of extra pocket money by going round each of the local football grounds after matches and picking up the results for the sports sections of the papers – after playing for his own team, of course. Barry and a mate managed to scrape together a few quid to get their hands on an old motorcycle and, in scenes probably familiar to older readers, ▶

they thrashed that old bike round a field building the skills that would serve Briggo well as a racer and motorcycle competitor.

Former wonderkid Moore had been one of Briggo's cycle speedway team-mates and had moved on to motorcycle speedway, then gone to England to race. A year later he was back and driving round in an Italian sports car so when one of the local engineering factories – also an exhaust maker – created a proper speedway track at the back of its premises and offered a couple of bikes for anyone who wanted to have a go, Barry was more than willing to try and emulate his friend.

What Briggo lacked in finances at that time he made up for in determination, and despite having to cycle two hours to reach the practice track and not having the sixpence a lap it cost to try speedway he knuckled in and was the pit mechanic/ helper for everyone. A bike needed a flat fixing, Barry was the lad; someone needed a pusher, up stepped Briggo; someone needed refuelling, well, you get the picture.

Even after 60 years or more Barry still grins at this: "I took all the hassle because my pay for doing it was 10 free laps each session and I'd also get to watch other techniques to help formulate my own style." Barry dreamed up a way to get into the

RIGHT: Left to right: Ove Fundin, Barry Briggs and Aub Lawson hold the winged wheel in 1958.

Arunui Speedway pits by doing basically the same job at Christchurch's track as he had at the training one. "I got hold of a pair of white overalls, stood at the entrance to the pits and offered to help any rider who needed it. I'd carry kit, tools, push bikes, anything, it sounds menial but I was in the thick of things in the track," he continued. Things hopped up a level when Charlie Roscoe, the owner of a lemonade factory and occasional sponsor, offered Barry the chance to try one of his bikes. "Problem was I had no real race kit, so I cut up an old pair of jodhpurs to use as a pattern, my mum got hold of some material somehow and a pair of race leathers were formed. It's lucky speedway wasn't too fashion-conscious at the time," he grinned. Racing boots were

created from an old pair of football boots, and a local racer took pity on him and loaned him a helmet. It was an inauspicious start to his career, and it was nearly finished before it began, with doubts about the padding in his leathers after a spill in the final session.

"I cured that by adding some carpet underlay to vulnerable points such as my knees," he said. "I thought there might be a problem with the leathers as there was a rule in New Zealand speedway that before you could race you had to prove you could lay the bike down safely on the track. Charlie wouldn't let me lay down one of his bikes, so I got this old Harley 'Peashooter' model from the 30s and did a lap or two on that then laid it down to satisfy the officials."

LIVING THE DREAM

Barry progressed quite quickly, made it into one of the local teams and that opened up other tracks for him to ride on. His burning ambition, however, was to race in England just like Ronnie had. "Two quid a week at an ad agency wasn't going to get me to England in a hurry, so a mate got me a job at an abattoir which paid a bit more in bonuses and all of a sudden the £85 fare was feasible." Though he'd expected to be heading for third division Aldershot, there were some frantic telegraph communications while he

> *Two quid a week at an ad agency wasn't going to get me to England in a hurry, so a mate got me a job at an abattoir which paid a bit more in bonuses and all of a sudden the £85 fare was feasible.*

was on the boat and instead 17-year-old Barry was on his way to Wimbledon – a first division team. Despite having no bike of his own, and only homemade leathers to race in, he was there. The loan of a spare track bike got him mobile, but as he was number eight rider the team mechanics were often too busy to do anything to his machine.

"I didn't really know any better and just rode it as it was, then Ronnie Moore suffered a breakdown with his bike and borrowed ▶

BELOW: If your job is racing motorcycles that's what you do… wherever it is.

mine for the last race. He went from winning to struggling to be third just because the bike was so bad," Barry recalls. "I started doing my own preparation after that." His fortunes improved a little when he was a regular team man, and as his first season came to an end he'd managed three fully paid maximum meetings but is the first to admit he had Moore watching his back. "Ronnie kept the other guys out of the way once I'd got to the front." The talent was clearly there and, however they came, so were the first wins which gave Barry the 'I can beat the top guys' mentality needed to achieve sustained success.

Briggo improved so rapidly that by 1954 he would place sixth in his first world final, and was also enjoying the fruits of travelling overseas series from his UK base. Looking for a first world title, Team Briggo made rapid inroads ahead of the event the following year and Barry was widely favoured to do well – but in the end though it was to be diminutive Peter Craven's evening, and Barry was left to ponder on a series of circumstances that left him third. A replacement big-end on his JAP motor started to break up, and while it would last a little longer the motor got sicker and sicker. There were options to use back-up bikes but Barry didn't, he stuck with his own ailing kit. "I rued that decision, but that's racing," he said. Barry explained that he'd also had a bit of bother on the track: "Another rider

brought me off in the run-off to determine second and third places. I was sitting in the track, 50 yards from the finish, feeling a bit sorry for myself. The other guy was picking his bike up and trying to start it, but hadn't pulled back on compression so it wouldn't have it. I got my act together, fired my bike up and rode over the line to take third spot."

In between this sobering experience at the world final and the run-up to the next one, Barry had a life-changing experience when he married June Elizabeth Rashbrook – Junie. It was something Briggo would regard as the proudest day of his life and his greatest success, and clearly they were good for each other. Their marriage produced two boys, Gary and Tony, and lasted until Junie died from cancer in December 2003.

CHAMPION OF THE WORLD
Competitors in top-level sport, particularly motorcycle racing, rarely reach the top by being shy and retiring given the inevitable flare-ups and personality clashes that will develop. Briggo has certainly never lacked determination, but has managed to measure this with a sense of fair play – and it's a combination that stood him in good stead at the 1957 world final when he was in the run-off with Ove Fundin. Gating faster than Briggs, Fundin took the lead but Barry knew he could catch him – and he did so by the third lap. Remember these laps are measured

ABOVE: Hands-on work from the legend while the rest watch on for tips.

in scant seconds, Briggo had been right on the Swede's tail… now they were elbow to elbow as they went into the turn. Barry was on the inside, sticking to the white line, Fundin had to go faster than he expected to try to get round the outside and Briggo – with more speed on than Fundin – went in low and Fundin went off. "I didn't dare move out from the line while Ove was crowding me," Barry said. "In the end he paid the price and I was world champion."

Being the defending title-holder, Briggo was automatically in the 1958 final and once again it was down to him and Fundin. For a second year running Barry came out on top, becoming only the second rider in speedway history to successfully defend his title – the first being Jack Young. Given the impressive feat, Barry felt he had additional bargaining power, but failed to reach an agreement with his team promoter about the return fare from New Zealand. There were supposedly strict rules about payments to racers and the boat fare of £280 was £30 more than the upper limit. The team refused to pay the difference and Barry 'retired' from speedway on a matter of principle, but it wasn't a hiatus that would last long once he got an offer from New Cross. The Briggs clan duly moved back to London, and then a year later – after a transfer to Southampton – they put down roots in the New Forest area. ▶

There's a case for Briggo being the ultimate all-rounder as he wasn't just successful in speedway. Here he is at a muddy scramble displaying his usual determination.

Times were good, and Barry even set up a speedway business when – having won a third world title in Sweden in 1964 – he agreed to ride ESO/Jawas, a make not exactly popular in the UK. Not only did he sign to ride for them, he also became the marque's speedway importer and set up shop in the railway arches in Southampton. "In retrospect, the fact I was selling stuff to riders I was racing against wasn't the best of ideas as they'd come up to me almost on the start line and ask for bits," he remembers. However, Briggo persevered and was soon winning again – this time for a fourth world championship win, the first for Jawa, once again in Sweden. He'd taken a considerable amount of time away from his business to concentrate solely on racing, and it obviously paid off both for Barry and Jawa which thanks to Barry's endeavours had gone from a 'funny foreign thing' viewed with suspicion to the motor of choice for all. Barry went on to say the success of the Jawa motor was down to its toughness,

and the fact the bikes held their value so riders were able to earn without it costing them a great deal. He added that one notable rider, Terry Betts, went for 18 meetings maintaining a top average points score – hardly touching the motor in all that time. And Barry hadn't just put Jawa on the map, his efforts gaining mainstream attention for the sport of speedway itself. He recalls: "We were having a great time; it was a popular sport again, exciting to watch and the TV companies were beginning to notice it." A measure of how popular it was, and more to the point how well known Barry had become, was in evidence at the prestigious BBC Sports Personality of the Year of 1966. As a world champion Barry got an automatic invitation to attend the show, but no one expected a motorcycle rider to be popular. Confounding expectations, he finished as runner-up – beaten only by football's World Cup-winning team captain Bobby Moore.

The desire to be competitive and win never leaves a top-level competitor, and approaching his 20th season Barry still felt he was capable of claiming a fifth world crown. He prepared well for his 1972 title attempt and took three months away from his business to concentrate on becoming both physically and mentally prepared for the task at hand. Earlier in his career he'd just go out and race as fast as he could, but with age creeping up on him part of Barry's preparation was to have a detailed plan on how he was going to win. His fellow New Zealander Ivan Mauger (in fact, a fellow native of Christchurch) was the favourite to win the championship that year, but Briggo realised he could beat Ivan if he could be first off the line. Barry's strategy involved some sportsmanship; Ivan would like to come to the line after everyone else had lined up to try and unnerve riders, but this time Briggo gave Mauger a taste of his own medicine

ABOVE: The man where he is happiest: out on the track, racing.

ABOVE: Here's what the well-dressed MXer will be wearing this season. Briggo broadslides an ESO MXer... or maybe lays it down.

BELOW: Briggo was always up for a challenge, and there are few more challenging things than riding a vintage Douglas up a hill climb...

before focusing on the green light. The tapes went up and Briggo was away with Mauger trailing behind. Things were looking good but, having made another good start in the next heat, the Swede Bernt Persson appeared behind Barry and wiped him – taking off part of his hand in the process. The race was stopped, medics rushed to Briggo's aid and he was carted off to hospital to have his hand operated on. It still rankles with him, 40 years on, that his crack at a fifth world title ended in this way.

MORE THAN JUST A RACER

As he explained, introducing the Jawa into the speedway scene wasn't the only thing Briggo was noted for: "I'm an inveterate tinkerer. I've got to be doing something to my bike and many times this meant I hadn't a clue what it was going to be like on the track. Jack Milne, who had won two world titles before I'd even landed in the UK, told me he rode virtually the same spec bike in all his career, never changed a thing. He knew exactly what that machine would do at any given time." But Barry's tinkering led him down plenty of interesting avenues. For instance, one of his pet hates was to see meetings rained off or riders hurt because dirt would be thrown up into their faces. His answer was a dirt deflector and from being an object of scorn they're now fitted to every bike. "It was just an idea," he said. Barry was also a skilled promoter, recognising the value of publicity and 'selling' yourself to the crowd or the organisers and when he decided to try the American scene he did it with aplomb by entering the Daytona flat track meeting as 'the world's fastest flat tracker'. "I'd no idea if I was the fastest flat tracker, but it sounded good," he laughed. "I took along an ice bike complete with spikes in the tyres and wiped four seconds off their lap record. That got me a ride at Madison Square Garden for an indoor meeting on concrete. I was partnered with Kenny Roberts for that meet, it got a bit exciting when I was accused of jumping the start, there was a bit of a discussion and I was shoved back on the third row. When the tapes went up I was first into the first corner with both feet down, there were guys and bikes everywhere, officials yelling, riders cursing and the crowd going wild. Great fun!"

It's impossible to talk about Barry Briggs in just a few pages, we've hardly touched on anything other than his speedway career. No mention of his diamond and gold mining, his mentoring of his sons' speedway racing, his prepping a motor for Japanese speedway, his attempt to run an ESO motor backwards to find more grip, or any of the countless other activities he's been involved with throughout the years. So, I can only suggest you get hold of a copy of his book and have a read... you might need a safety helmet though, it's a wild ride.

Just as I was packing up to leave Barry to his development of golf clubs (another of his schemes) he looked at me and said: "If you could write your life in pencil and rub bits out, I wouldn't."

Chapter 5

ABOVE: A small test of observation here – spot the worn crank pin…

TOP LEFT: Magneto timing and operation is modified in a Godden 'Gold Top' engine.

TOP MIDDLE: Even valve guides can be usefully modified to increase reliability and power.

TOP RIGHT: Cam followers get the polishing and relieving treatment, too. It's all about stress release.

Don Godden

Top grass and long track racer Don Godden was interviewed for *The Motor Cycle* in 1968 to see just how he managed to make a 35-year-old engine design work so well…

For an engine designed in the 1930s to still be the choice of a racer determined to win in the then 'modern' era of 1968, the basic concept of that engine must have been pretty good. At that time, *The Motor Cycle's* man Vic Willoughby visited multi-time British grass track champion and talented engineer Don Godden to find out what the lad did to make those engines work way beyond the maker's wildest expectations.

Immediately he found there were remarkably few changes from its inception to the latest 1960s model. The crankcases were cast in the magnesium alloy known by its trade name of Elektron, the con rod was either in Duralumin – another trade name – or steel. Willoughby went as far as to say the drawing used in the feature was an updated one from the 1930s and all the artist had to do was to erase the track carburettor and replace it with a Concentric carburettor, shorten the cylinder and con rod a little and erase a pushrod return spring. The feature went on to say the speedway JAP had the right sort of power to propel a speedway bike and rider off the line in the best time possible. That this power was flagging at a little more than 5000rpm, and all but gone at 6000rpm, was of little matter to a race on a track of 440 yards. The JAP motor was, while not the only one in use, dominating the speedway scene.

When the race track was 1000 metres long, however, it was a different kettle of fish and with the standard JAP motor Godden barely had enough power to qualify when he made his early forays into the scene in Germany.

Clearly something had to be done and he set about it with a good measure of common sense, engineering talent and a deal of determination. He did it to such good effect that three years later he was challenging for the top spot in the longer format. This, thought Willoughby, was a story worth hearing and detailing in the paper. With a grass track career going back as far as 1953 Godden had earned himself nine British championships using equipment he'd built himself, and latterly by co-operating with Alf Hagon to provide a commercial JAP tuning service. This was the basis of the motor Willoughby went along to hear about. In 1968 the basic JAP speedway motor was available for £140, however for another £30 Godden/Hagon would provide a 'Gold Top' engine, likely a reference to the gold top milk which was extra creamy and had foil in gold rather than silver; the 'Gold Top' JAP was reckoned to be the cream of the crop. To distinguish their high-performance engine from the rest, Godden and Hagon had the rocker covers anodised yellow – it's just a shame the effect can't be seen in black and white photos.

Starting with the standard JAP motor, Godden first addressed the cam timing which went from the inlet opening at 45 degrees before TDC, and closing at 62 degrees after BDC – the exhaust opening at 65 degrees before BDC, and closing

BELOW: When fettled to his exacting standards, Don's JAPs were a match for the foreign competition on the long tracks of Europe.

JAP

REG. TRADE·MARK

ABOVE: These poor things have a tough life in a race engine.

BELOW: Lining up the flywheels before tightening the crank pin nuts.

ABOVE: In an ultra-high compression engine there is the danger of valves hitting the piston crown. This is bad, so those that know what they're doing relieve the valve pock so if it does tangle it's square on and doesn't bend the val

With spreader bolts opened out to create some tension, a sharp tap on the crank pin will split the flywheels.

ABOVE: Godden made his own special cogs for various applications.

at 35 degrees after TDC. Using his own cam grinding jig Godden altered these timings to 60, 85, 90 and 55, vastly increasing the overlap, but this on its own wasn't enough and modifying one part of an engine has an effect on other areas. What was likely to happen with such modification to the cam timing would be the majority of the increased fresh charge coming into the cylinder would be pushed straight out the exhaust valve unless the port shape was changed. Willoughby reported that Godden's handiwork in the inlet port prevented this from happening. Other work, aimed at stopping valve float at high revs, included progressive rate valve springs and alloy pushrods rather than steel. With a motor now safe to 7000rpm rather than 6000rpm it was a useful increase in performance for the expert rider who it was reckoned could quite easily cope with the slight loss of flexibility from the modified unit.

Even this performance-enhancing work wasn't enough for Godden's 1000-metre engines, and the work needed to make the venerable JAP cut it with the opposition in Europe amounted to major surgery. Gone was any semblance of power below 4000rpm, but in its place was reliable power way beyond the 7000rpm of the 'Gold Top' motor. To achieve this, Godden has a seriously wild cam profile that increased the valve lift by 50% and needed flat-grinding on the valves' edges or they would tangle at high speed. Allied to this extra lift, the inlet port was opened out from 1⅛ to 1⅜ which needs an Amal GP carb with twin-float chambers to feed in the fuel. Naturally, Godden felt the standard Dural con rod was not quite right for this wild engine and used a steel one.

At this level of competition the search for extra performance is intense; any little increase in power is welcome and anything which prevents power loss is worth investigating. For instance, though important for providing sparks to the plug a magneto can absorb power. Okay, only a little power, but far better it be available for race winning than

LEFT: There is often a limit on how much lift a big valve can have before something touches. The flat on the rim means the valves miss.

not. Apparently running the magneto at quarter engine speed rather than half engine speed releases that absorbed power.

JAP WRINKLES

When interviewing Godden for the earlier feature, Willoughby realised there was a vast amount of untapped information on making a JAP engine work to the best of its ability. He also, in conversation with Don, realised that while not everyone wanted to super-tune an engine to howl it round the European long tracks there were an awful lot of enthusiasts who wanted to go grass tracking, second-half speedway riding, hill climbing and sprinting with the engine and they would benefit from knowing how to screw the unit together. So, the pair collaborated and produced a 'how to' feature for the 500cc JAP motor.

A lot of the work was under the heading 'common sense', but even so it doesn't hurt to go back to basics with such things. For the basis of this, and indeed all such features, it has to be assumed the reader attempting to follow the advice has a work space, tools and some knowledge. Taking each part of the engine in turn, Godden related his experiences of the robust unit and how it holds up in service.

All case faces are prepared so they mate fully and prevent leaks.

ABOVE: Each cam is for a different purpose, with grass, sand and long tracks requiring slightly different power.

high lift cams which would need the valve pockets deepening so the valves didn't clout the piston on full lift. Also a departure from JAP practice was the closing-up of the ring gaps. Most people will know the piston rings form part of the sealing of the combustion process, and the ring gap is an important part of that. Too big a gap and the engine burns oil, too small a gap and the ring ends will touch when the engine is hot and seize. Using alcohol as a fuel means the engine runs a lot cooler, and Don found a smaller gap worked perfectly.

Naturally with a man dedicated to performance, there were also a few tips of use to those working on a budget and if replacing standard cams with high performance ones isn't viable then perhaps Godden's ingenious method of grinding back the rocker pad on the arm may be of interest. Also, Godden's method of timing the ignition is sure to create some discussion; he did it by ear!

BELOW: If you think logically about how many times the rockers open and close a valve and how heavy they are as standard, then lightening them makes sense as it gives all other components an easy time.

Taking the crankcases first the main bearings run in steel rings, Elecktron not being an ideal material for the housing. These rings should be a good fit in the case, but if there's any suggestion of main shaft misalignment on the crank then this can loosen the rings. Godden suggested Araldite adhesive to tighten them up again. On the main bearings Godden advised it was best to renew them each racing season or problems would occur. Also, the crank pin had a limited racing life and the advice here was to junk it after 25 meetings. The pin is where the big end runs and has a hardened surface for the rollers. Under racing conditions this surface breaks up and all sorts of nasty things can happen. If the big end has failed then the cause must be investigated or it will happen again – it could be the oil feed, or a blockage somewhere.

To replace the crank pin – and this is an indication of how enthusiasts seemed to be much more practical 50 years ago because these days the crank would be shipped off to a specialist – the article advised to hold the

ABOVE: Don aimed to have the crank running as true as possible. If they're not then the ride can be uncomfortable and it's not good for race-winning power, plus the engine can shake itself to bits.

flywheel by clamping a large spanner in a vice, sit the crank nut in it and heave on the other but with a socket ground to remove the lead in radius. Then use three bolts to put pressure on the inside of the flywheels and then fix an old crank pin to the original and give the end a sharp tap to release the taper. As time goes on the flywheel tapers can enlarge, so JAP provided oversize crank pins to cope with this and allow the proper side float of the rod to be achieved. Assembling was regarded as a simple task merely requiring a new crank pin to be bolted in place, the rod with new bearing rollers fitted then the other flywheel fitted and the whole lot bolted up with new nuts. Any misalignment found in the truing jig was cured by bumping the assembly on a stout surface with a sheet of soft metal in place. Willoughby suggested the balance factor should really be checked, though only as a courtesy as it was unlikely to be far out – but you can bet Godden always checked his.

Godden stepped away from standard JAP practice and used a Mahle piston with a thicker crown which was useful for coping with

ABOVE: Clean and tidy, not overly glitzy, and blisteringly fast... a bit like the rider really.

FROM THE ARCHIVE

This summary of Willoughby's work isn't intended to be a workshop manual – nor was the original feature, come to that – but it just goes to demonstrate the way a successful racer known for his meticulous preparation operated. The following four pages are the original text of another article on Don Godden – this time from *Motor Cycle Weekly* – and if there's anything to be learned from either of these profiles it's that if you want the best ideas, listen to someone who's been winning.

Godden Engineering

Faced with a dwindling share of Weslake business, Don Godden takes the bull by the horns and designs an ohc four-valver – the GR500.

Former multiple grass and long track champion Don Godden, still racing after 25 years, chooses *Motor Cycle Weekly* for the first announcement of his own four-valver. Overhead camshaft, with choice of cams and compression ratios, blends speedway torque with long track speed. Fits any frame. Robust and simple to service. £20,000 investment. Spring debut planned.

Britain's strength in the speedway, grass track and long track markets – restored so emphatically these last four years by the Weslake four-valve pushrod engine – gets another great boost as Don Godden steals London's Racing and Sporting Show with his GR500 overhead-camshaft four-valver on Stand 10 in the Old Horticultural Hall.

Ironically, it was Godden who first put the Weslake message across with a spectacular performance in the Lydden international grass track meeting in October 1974. Such was the engine's superiority that four-valve conversions blossomed like buttercups in May and Jawa and JAP were forced to double up their valve gear. Competition had never been so fierce.

Conversions apart, Godden's GR500 is the fourth major four-valver in the last four years and its prospects are surely the rosiest. Not only is it backed by 25 years' experience on the tracks and 20 years in the tuning and manufacturing business; it also has a chain-driven overhead camshaft, to give it the extra power and reliability at sustained high rpm for long track without sacrificing the four-valver's characteristic torque for speedway.

What's more, it slots into any Jawa, Weslake or Godden frame and accepts a Weslake exhaust pipe and induction manifold.

Godden's confidence in the new project is shown by a £20,000 investment in a Bridgeport Series 1 CNC (computerised, numerically controlled) milling machine, to be installed next month in his works at East Mailing, Kent.

And such is his reputation for quality and sound design that he has already taken 20 firm orders, even though he has tried to keep the project secret until now.

Don's ambition to produce his own engine goes back to the time when he set up his JAP tuning business 20 years ago, though it was still only vague when he was invited to Czechoslovakia in 1972 to help Jawa adapt its speedway two-valver to long track racing.

But though that collaboration resulted in long track titles for Ivan Mauger, Ole Olsen and Barry Briggs, Jawa couldn't supply Don with the engines he wanted for the frames he was marketing.

CHALLENGE

Back in Britain, Godden twisted an arm or two at AMC and BSA in the hope of inspiring a British challenge to the Jawa. But he drew a blank until Weslake took the hint.

As one of the first two distributors (Dave Nourish was the other), Don initially handled half Weslake's speedway production. But as more and more agents were appointed his share dwindled below what he needed to market the track machines for which he already made the frames, forks and gearboxes himself. That was the spur that finally crystallised his engine-building ambition. Drawing started in August.

Godden's vast all-round experience as a rider had convinced him the engine must be simple to service in the field. And his professional tuning experience had taught him the weaknesses of other engines and the limitations of pushrods for long track.

Hence the overhead camshaft; the choice of materials for their suitability rather than their cost; the generous dimensions of shafts and bearings; and the accent on ease of maintenance, including practically foolproof timing of valves and ignition.

Simplicity is evident in the basic layout as well as in servicing – the engine has only two shafts, because the oil pump is driven by the crankshaft and the contact breaker by the camshaft.

Supplied by Kent Automotive Castings, the well-known racing specialists in Sittingbourne, the crankcase is in LM25, an aluminium alloy of high strength and low expansion. Besides the usual webs radiating from the main bearing housings, it has a cluster of close-pitch stiffening fins front and rear and extends more than 2⅜ inches up the cylinder.

There is a hole high in the left-hand wall for locating top dead centre with a rod pushed through into a corresponding flywheel hole.

Made of EN4OB (a nitriding steel), the flywheels have the mainshafts pressed in from left and right in the usual way. But these shafts are not only in high-quality EN36, they are also 10% larger than usual – 1.1in (28mm) against 1in (25mm) – to prevent their taking a set in the wheels when the compression ratio is bumped up.

The two main bearings are Dürkopp caged needle rollers and there is a hardened and ground thrust washer each side for flywheel location.

There are no nuts on the crankpin, the wheels being pressed hard against

ABOVE: The camshaft vernier comprises 12 holes in sprocket, 13 in hub and a locking plate with integral peg.

the shoulders. Pin diameter in the middle is 1.403in (35.64mm) and the Alfa big-end bearing comprises 13 caged pairs of 6mm-diameter rollers – each pair being of unequal length (6mm and 8mm) staggered to prevent a ridge from forming round the middle of the pin.

OPTION

Material of the forged connecting rod is optional with no price difference. Light alloy is recommended for performance but anyone with a lingering preference for steel may have it, though renewal after a year's racing is advised in either case.

In the small end, the con rod has a Vandervell steel-backed phosphor-bronze bush. Also a KAC casting in LM25, the cylinder has 6½in square finning and a cast-iron liner shrunk in. Made to Godden's design, the Omega forged piston has a full skirt, two plain rings (0.8mm and 1mm thick) and a flat

ABOVE: Points to note: Left – steep downdraught angle, contact-breaker housing (top), oil-pump housing (bottom), cam-chain tensioner and oil-collector box. Right – splined sprocket carrier and timing hole in crankcase wall.

ARCHIVE FEATURE 1979: A TALE OF DEDICATION

crown with recesses for the valve heads.

Crown height governs compression ratio; 13:1 is recommended for speedway while 15:1 is the maximum for long track.

Standard bore and stroke are 85.5mm x 86mm (494cc) but there is provision for three oversizes – 0.010, 0.015 and 0.020in. The largest of these brings the bore to 86mm for a capacity of 499cc.

Cast by the Pelican foundry in Gillingham, the head is in LM25 with austenitic-iron seat rings shrunk in for the valves. Angle included by the stems is 40 degrees and the 10mm NGK plug is bang in the middle.

Squish turbulence is provided by a close-clearance band all round the combustion chamber and Honda-style segment front and rear. Downdraught angle is 28 degrees,

while the horizontal exhaust port is inclined 15 degrees to the right and takes a pipe of 1⅛in outside diameter.

Inlet port diameter is 27mm at the flange, while the overall valve diameters are 33½mm inlet, 28½mm exhaust.

Carburettor size (Amal or Gardner) is 36mm and both straight and angled manifolds are available to suit frame layout. For international events, of course (though not for grass track or British League speedway) a 34mm double-taper restrictor is provided for clamping between carburettor and manifold to suit the FIM rule.

Supported in large and small ball bearings, the camshaft is in EN36 with integral lobes. It is driven direct from the crankshaft by a ⅜in-pitch flat-sided German Jwis (pronounced Eevis) roller chain – a make Godden has been racing for the past two years.

The front run of the chain is damped by a rubbing strip in HMWP (high molecular weight polyethylene) while the rear run is tensioned by an adjustable curved blade in the same material. Sprocket sizes are 17-tooth (crankshaft) and 34-tooth (camshaft) and there is a vernier timing adjustment at the top.

ABOVE: In the crankcase halves are the Dürkopp main bearings and one of the thrust washers. Mainshafts are massive. Con rod here is steel. Outboard of camchain sprocket is slotted oil-pump drive. Cylinder casting incorporates chain tunnel.

Three cam forms are available. The most tractable gives opening and closing points of 60/80 degrees (inlet) and 80/40 degrees exhaust, and is set up with the inlet valve fully open 98 degrees after TDC.

Each rocker runs on a pair of Torrington needle roller bearings on a $^7/_{16}$in hardened and ground spindle. The cam followers (patent applied for) are ¾in-diameter rollers on tiny needle bearings. A leverage ratio of 1.18:1 in the rocker arms gives a valve lift of 0.375in.

To time the valves in the field, the engine is simply set at TDC and the camshaft turned until the valve springs automatically settle it in the middle of the overlap period, before fitting the chain.

Godden has laid the head out to provide room for Terry's double-coil valve springs about 50% larger in diameter than those in the Weslake. As a result, torsional stresses in the wire are only two-thirds as high. In conjunction with the lighter reciprocating weight, this should ensure freedom from valve float in the severest long track race.

The Lucas contact breaker is

LEFT: Though the cylinder head is on-machined here, the annular squish band and two segments can be clearly seen. Head joint is sealed by a copper gasket, chain tunnel by an O-ring.

claims it will obviate the cavitation and inconsistent delivery he has experienced with other plunger pumps at high engine speeds.

O-rings are used to seal the contact breaker and the chain-tunnel joints at top and bottom of the cylinder. Eight bolts clamp the crankcase halves and four long studs secure the cylinder and head. As usual, the engine-sprocket carrier provides for slight sideways movement of the sprocket on splines.

Engine weight, says Godden, should be 2lb lighter than a Jawa, 2lb heavier than a Weslake. Inflation makes costs more difficult to pinpoint but at today's levels the engine should sell for about £650.

The production schedule is for 100 engines this year and 200-300 a year thereafter. Godden is aiming to have the first four running by March. One will be for his personal use, one for top grass tracker Graham Hurry, one for speedway and the other for evaluation abroad.

Like any other engine, the GR500 will be judged on results. But, considering Godden's experience and high standards, its ultimate performance seems a foregone conclusion.

driven by a male taper on the right-hand end of the camshaft. Standard advance (fixed) is 35 degrees.

Total-loss lubrication is by a worm-driven Silk pump working in a sealed chamber in the right-hand crankcase half. Oil from this chamber is forced up the hollow mainshaft to the big end. A smaller feed goes through internal drillways to the cylinder head, where it squirts on the cam lobes before being splashed round from a well beneath them.

In typical speedway fashion, oil draining into the crankcase is flung into a collector box at the rear and blown out to atmosphere.

Since the Silk pump has a drive reduction of 35:1 (instead of the usual 24:1) and a more positive valve mechanism (using plungers, not balls), Godden

Rotrax Jawa

It's all clean and tidy. Rotrax was just one of many frame builders who supplied the speedway market and originally was a bicycle maker. It still is, in fact.

TOP LEFT CLOCKWISE: Remove a circlip, slip the sprocket off (then a new one on), clip on the circlip, faster gear ratio changes.

Two alloy stampings welded together make up the fuel tank.

Slim and small to allow the rider to move around.

Intake bell-mouth provides a smoother air flow and some form of air filtration.

Typical of bikes being raced in the late 1960s and early 1970s is this Rotrax. Although it was possible to buy speedway machines ready to go, many racers assembled their own from favourite parts; or rather, updated their chassis with a more modern motor, as is the case with this Rotrax-type Jawa. It would have originally been supplied with a JAP engine through Alec Jackson, who took on the speedway engine side of JA Prestwich in the 1950s.

The Rotrax company grew out of the foundations laid by a man called Bill Harvell, a competition cyclist who was talented enough to win a medal in the cycling events of the 1932 Olympic Games. Southampton-based, and with a reputation for quality workmanship, the small concern was taken over and expanded in 1945 when the Rotrax name emerged. A diversion into speedway came in 1952 when its first track-race frame was produced using top-quality Reynolds 531 tube superbly brazed in its workshops. An instant hit, the frame was popular among riders and like a lot of popular things, it was copied in small workshops to feed the scene – so, what is referred to as 'Rotrax' isn't always Rotrax.

Once the JAP engines began to be outclassed by the eastern European makers it was a simple enough thing to slot the

LEFT: When weight is the enemy there's nothing more lightweight than a hole – as in the sprocket lightening holes. No reason it can't be a cool shape, though.

BELOW: Massive engine plates hold everything in place and stiffen the light chassis considerably.

A distinctly modern-looking Rotrax frame from the 1950s or possibly the 60s, and a 1972 two-valve Jawa engine slotted in.

A leading-axle front wheel provides better turning control for broadsliding.

ABOVE: Norton's three-spring clutch was a popular fitting for speedway bikes, it was tough and worked.

two-valve Jawa into the chassis – well, simple so long as you could cut alloy sheet accurately. It still has the Martin countershaft box with an AMC/Norton three-spring clutch fitted and Rotrax concealed spring front forks with bushes, rather than bearings in the steering head of the early Mk 1 chassis. We only know it's an early chassis because it still has an external oil tank, while later Mk 2 frames carried the oil in the frame tubes.

The lubrication system is total-loss, and an external Pilgrim-type pump bolted to the side of the engine pushes the castor oil round the important bits. Making the spark is the job of a front-mounted magneto and helping the thirsty motor get its fair share of dope is a 900 series Amal carburettor. The air filter is angled so the rider's leg doesn't obscure the intake and cut down on the air flow.

In the early Rotrax series the rear wheel would be of 22-inch diameter but following a change of regulation the sizes dropped to 19 inches on the rear for the later frames, a size which remains to this day.

ABOVE: With no gear changing to be done there's no need for a fancy gearbox – the Martin countershaft provides enough to hang a clutch and drive sprocket on.

RIGHT: Mixing the 1970s motor with an earlier frame works in the speedway world.

EMBASSY
INTERNATIONALE

Wimbledon Stadium
Mon 29th May 1978
7·45 pm

Souvenir
Programme 25p

W.D. & H.O. WILLS

SPONSOR OF SPORT

HANG ON THERE, CHUM...

At first glance this looks rather like an attempt to handicap a fast lad by some slower riders, but no. It is actually a test of race clutch. Everyone knows the drill at the start of a current speedway heat; four racers line up in the gate, clutches in, engines revving, the tapes fly up, clutches are engaged and off they go. So intrinsic is this to the sport that it seems it must always have been that way – but that's not the case. At the dawn of the sport these speedway chaps had a rolling start and strict instructions to arrive at the line together then race off. This apparently led to some interesting scenes, and in an attempt to make things fairer and safer the governing body decided clutches were needed.

Our picture is from early 1933 and shows the West Ham team hanging on to the back of a team bike to try and make the clutch fail in their pre-season training. There was a sense of urgency as clutch starts were to become compulsory and such scenes would be common at all tracks during this time.

Chapter 6

Weslake's Rye factory

Before Don Godden's GR500 breakthrough, there was another British name practising engineering excellence...

In at the beginning, Stewart Boroughs, centre, sees the first step in the designing of the Weslake two-valve head. On the left is director David Short.

B arring one or two exceptions – CCM and Silk being the examples which spring to mind – the late 1970s saw a steady decline in the British motorcycle industry both in terms of the number of manufacturers and the motorcycles being produced. There was, however, one outstanding success story to emerge – that of Weslake.

In a little more than three years after the engine was first planned, Weslake's four-valver had taken over the market which had ruled for the previous 10 years by the Czechoslovakian giant Jawa. The company, based in the quiet Sussex town of Rye, then progressed from innovative design and development of the engine to attempting to produce the complete speedway racing machine. In 1976, *The Motor Cycle's* Stewart Boroughs visited the Weslake factory to find out more, and the following pages present the original words and images from the article he produced as a result.

**ARCHIVE FEATURE 1976:
THE WESLAKE RACER**

Weslake expands

Output doubled over next year

S uch has been the meteoric success of Weslake's engine in speedway – only 16 months have passed since England captain John Louis first tested a prototype on the shale at Hackney

Wick – that Weslake has been unable to meet the unprecedented demand for engines and spares.

To give the old-established, small family firm the capacity to meet this demand and expansion for making complete machines, production of its eight-valve twin-cylinder, in 500cc, 750cc and 850cc versions, has passed to its northern distributor Dave Nourish. Demand for the twin is still strong, particularly from continental grass track riders, and Nourish, with all the tools, jigs, spares and parts moved from Rye within the last three weeks, will continue to make the engines and spares

LEFT: Part of a consignment of crankcase halves which come in batches of 40 from the foundry in London.

from his planned extended premises at Langham, Oakham, in Rutland.

The space made available at Rye has allowed the speedway engine assembly shop to be tripled in size, and labour-saving automatic pegboard-type multipurpose drills, one a fixed spindle, and other special equipment are being installed.

Present labour force is 50 hourly-paid men plus 10 others, including chairman Harry Weslake himself, managing director Michael Daniel, co-directors David Short and Mrs Mary Weslake (who, by the way, used to ride a Brough Superior), and consultant engineer Ron Valentine. Harry Weslake, although 78, is still actively involved in the company and visits regularly.

The firm is based in four single-storey buildings on two acres of marshland near the harbour at Rye, and planning permission has been approved by the Rother District Council for a "substantial expansion" in the near future.

"Since April 15, 1975, something over 400 engines plus spares have

▶

ABOVE: First picture of one of the jigs for making the new Weslake frames. The job of bending and welding the frames will be subcontracted out. One hundred frames are planned in the first year.

BELOW: Just one of the new pieces of special equipment installed recently to increase production. This is an automatic pegboard multi-purpose drill.

been made," said director David Short. "Originally we had planned for 150 for the period so far this year. In fact, we've produced 250.

"We're now thinking in terms of 10 to 12 engines a week production, or in excess of 500 a year, about 100 of them incomplete machines, and the recent retooling and machinery in which we have invested something in the region of £50,000 over the last 18 months, should allow us to meet this projection with the present workforce."

Utilising the large extension, complete bikes will be assembled – 10 of everything from handlebars, seats, throttles, pairs of control levers to wheels are now at the factory.

Lengths of steel tubing for the frames, too, have already been delivered. They will weigh and be of a similar pattern as the Jawa, and jigs for bending and welding the tubing have arrived. But the bending and welding will be contracted out, then the complete frames returned for the bikes to be completed.

And in the engine assembly shop the extra space engenders a more streamlined, compact and efficient running unit with the quality control inspector now in the same room as the four fitters. Each hand-built engine takes approximately three hours to build from separated crankcases up.

As part of the much tighter quality control steps taken, there are air measuring gauges for quicker, more precise checking of things like big-end and small-end eyes in the con rods.

Being a small firm, a great deal of work is subcontracted out. About a dozen firms are needed to provide parts – valves, valve springs, oil pumps, gaskets, bearings, seals, forgings and the bulk of castings are prime examples.

And two of these imported parts have caused a number of engine failures. Last year it was found that piston weight had crept up causing expensive con rod failures in some cases. And more recently two or three crankpins are known to have caused damage.

"We realise there have been problems including failure in some parts. But you must bear in mind that the four-valver is a racing engine developed to win on the track. And no racer can be made 100% reliable and remain competitive. When problems materialise we modify and cure as they come up," said Short.

A small foundry was bought lock, stock and barrel from the north Kent area some six months ago and this supplies small batches of 10

ABOVE: A foundryman positions cylinder barrel moulds. Made of sand mixed with silicon of soda, the mould sets when carbon dioxide is passed through.

or a dozen castings – essential to Weslake for prototype work. But the bulk are made at the foundry in London.

"The general economic atmosphere has caused delays in keeping our three distributors – Don Godden and Reg Luckhurst in Kent; and our northern supplier, Dave Nourish in Rutland – in spares.

"In general firms ask for orders six months in advance, payment of 50% with the order and the rest on delivery.

"With pistons, for example, there are standard, +5, +10 and +20 sizes and it's all too easy to overestimate or underestimate an order. In our case, not foreseeing such a strong demand that developed from last September, the four sizes led to a shortage, particularly of piston rings.

"They are problems which we have to face, live with and improve upon where possible now that Weslake is in the speedway machine business."

Boffins at Rye are constantly scheming new ideas. As soon as

RIGHT: Another part of the more stringent checking. Here cam wheel tolerances are tested.

they heard of a possible ban on four-valvers in the sport their next project was to design a two-valve conversion to fit the present engine.

And neither is the 1000cc 50 degree V-twin superbike engine forgotten, based on two speedway engines. For the moment their own five- or six-speed gearbox will be fitted, with unit construction coming in the future possibly in 12 months. Crankcases are in the speedway assembly room and they are aiming to have an engine on display at the Earls Court Show in a few weeks' time.

England has the best opportunity in years of producing the world champion in 1976. All five English riders will be Weslake-mounted, including Weslake's teamsters Peter Collins, Malcolm Simmons and John Louis.

Aim is to have all three riders on the new Weslake for the final in Poland at Katowice on September 5. That would be a tremendous achievement, one of the trio taking the world title!

Production versions should be available before the end of the season and will cost between £700 and £800.

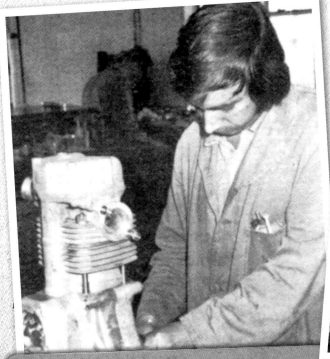

ABOVE: Effort in checking parts has more than doubled in the last year. Here the inspector checks the big-end eye of a con rod with the new air measuring gauges.

RIGHT: Each engine is hand-built and takes about three hours to assemble from the crankcase halves.

Five-valve Weslake

A case of what might have been but there it is, banned because of cost reasons, or that's what was said…

In striving to keep ahead of the opposition, Peter Collins tried a five-valve head on his Weslake… it was banned before he could race it.

ABOVE: With oil lines on the right-hand side they're out of harm's way should a rider have to lay the bike down.

LEFT: It stands for Brian Valentine Racing who worked with Weslake on the project.

ABOVE: How cool is that, a Castrol sticker with your picture on it…

RIGHT: Though the five-valve Weslake was bang up-to-date, it still had that 1930 feel to it.

BELOW: The carb is tucked away between seat tubes and the air filter is protected, too.

ABOVE: Things have moved on from the Norton clutch; more springs, more plates, better adjustment.

BELOW: Suspension was a little more sophisticated in later machines, but not that much more.

Sometimes a great idea is knocked on the head before it even gets a chance to prove itself. Such a fate befell the Weslake BVR five-valve engine designed and brought to fruition by Brian Valentine. The Valentine name had been associated with Weslake for a long time as Brian's father Ron was involved with the Weslake four-valve speedway engine put to such good use by Peter Collins, and many others besides. The development of the five-valve engine came about through the specific needs of the speedway scene and the desirability of torque in such engines. Brian had been impressed by the torque figures for Yamaha's FZR1000 with five-valves per cylinder, and reckoned such a motor would be just the thing to offer to speedway racers. After a lot of work and considerable expense he revealed his creation to the world, and promptly banned by the FIM for speedway. A few engines did indeed make it to the grass track scene and did prove the concept was correct. Former world speedway champion Peter Collins – also a dab hand on the grass – got hold of one of the few engines made and put it in a Weslake chassis (pictured here).

Explaining his concept to the press nearly 30 years ago, Valentine allowed there had been other attempts at a five-valve motor but they were plagued with high wear on the central valve guide, while his own engine design had eliminated this problem. So effective a design was Valentine's valve control that he was granted a patent on it soon after producing the system. Developing a chain-driven overhead cam single, Valentine pointed out the major advantage of a five-valve head is the larger potential inlet area at lower openings – thus providing more torque. The problem which had to be overcome was one of the inlet valves was expected to operate at a much steeper angle compared to the other two, and as previous attempts by engineers to make five-valve heads found this accelerated the wear considerably with valve guides lasting minutes. Valentine used a longer valve stem and offset the rocker arm so all side thrust on the stem was eliminated leading to a much happier time for the valve guide.

It is possible that such concerns over the high wear rate were behind the FIM banning the engine at the outset, Brian had his own thoughts on that when speaking to the press. The engine was capable of producing between 40bhp and 58bhp depending on the use, the fuel used and the actual configuration of the oiling system. It seems a great shame that it was banned.

Chapter 7

Peter Spencer Collins

British speedway world champions are a rare breed, and one such winner is Peter Collins who can recall his famous victory like it was yesterday...

It wasn't just speedway for Mr Collins, he may be on his way to a world title but grass track was still part of it. Here he is in action at the Grass Track GP in August 1976.

World champions don't just spring, fully formed, into their chosen sport and the road to the glamorous end of an activity such as speedway is often long and hard – but it has to start somewhere. For Peter Spencer Collins that starting point came on the family farm in 1962 as an eight-year-old when his dad cut down a 98cc James Comet by fitting wheels from a BSA Dandy so he could race it round a track worn in the fields. "Hardly the most glamorous motorcycle to start on," grinned Peter, "but I was mobile." He wasn't the only person enjoying himself in impromptu races in the fields of his father's farm. Some of the farmworkers would also be riding motorcycles around the same track and of course as time progressed other members of the Collins family would be joining elder brother Peter as they all learnt to drift and slide various machines. Peter was introduced to speedway as a sport when friends and family took him along to see the Belle Vue Aces. During our chat Peter said it was watching the track action of the team and its star man at that time, Peter Craven, which awakened the desire to go racing himself. With the Comet – now slightly bigger as he was getting older – providing the means to practise what he witnessed during the race nights, he began working on all sorts of different schemes in order to trade up to bigger and better machines. A lot of creative thinking went into earning the cash required to start racing, initially on the grass tracks of Cheshire. For instance, an after-school job at a market garden brought in two shillings an hour; bagging up horse manure earned a little. More official work started by then, too, as Peter began ▶

Not the most glamorous start for a future world champion, but Peter Collins became mobile on a James Comet just like this.

an apprenticeship at Shell Chemicals as a fitter and turner. With the regular wage packet and his earnings from the market garden he could not only afford to buy his first grass track race bike – a Hagon with the then-popular BSA C15 four-stroke single engine in it – but also a snazzy pair of blue leathers.

It seemed that the years of battling unsuitable bikes around the fields was going to pay off as Peter won his first race in 1970,

Grass track stardom awaited with the purchase of a Hagon C15 BSA similar to this one.

and carried on winning all through the season. He was invited along to Crewe speedway for its training sessions and second-half rides – second-half racing was the traditional way for youngsters to make their start in the sport – but he hadn't got a speedway bike. A grass racing friend's brother was involved at Crewe and offered the use of the spare track bike, but it failed to start for his first race so he went out on a full-on team bike. When the flag dropped,

young Mr Collins was first past it – and he did the same again later in the meeting and at a few subsequent meetings, too. People were starting to take notice of Peter, one in particular was Frodsham garage proprietor Jim Rowlinson who was known to sponsor local grass track racers. Jim told Peter he was going to sponsor him on the grass for the next season, and it would also be good if he went along to Belle Vue's speedway training sessions. It was a dream come true for Peter; a Belle Vue fan being offered the chance to race for his favourite team.

He would start the 1971 season with the Rochdale Hornets – a Belle Vue training team – but by the end of the year he was riding for the full squad and remained with them for the rest of his career. "I never wanted to ride for anyone else," he admitted.

Things were going well for Peter's race career and a 350 grass track championship came at the end of 1971, repeated in 1972, while he was also taken under the wing of Ivan Mauger who reckoned Collins would be a good addition to the Belle Vue speedway team. His earnings from racing were stacking up, and that allowed him to pay back the neighbour who generously loaned him the cash to buy his first proper speedway machine.

Though making a name for himself, Peter was still a part-timer and was holding down a full-time job at Shell. Like all teenage racers he felt himself to be indestructible and the workload was just something that went with his chosen sport. However, the realisation things might have to change came one memorable month when he raced at 32 meetings and still went into work each day. Peter recalled: "I was absolutely knackered, hardly able to keep my eyes open. When I stopped and thought about it I was earning more from racing than working so I 'retired' from work at 18 even though I enjoyed being a fitter and turner and the skills learnt have stood me in good stead."

The life of a racer might seem like a glamorous one, but the decision to give up a job – a career even – chasing something that's not guaranteed is not easy. Nor is actually doing it; the planning, the travelling, the commitment required – all of that potentially combined with a nine-to-five if the rider isn't quite in a position to rely solely on income from motorcycles. Peter's reflections on that time in his life are very matter of fact: "I wasn't the only one doing this. I'd be at Belle Vue on a Saturday evening, a mate would drive my bikes to Germany, after racing I'd get the sleeper from Manchester's Piccadilly to Euston Station, taxi to Heathrow, fly to Germany for a Sunday afternoon long or grass track, back to the UK for say Monday night at Reading, then drive up to Leicester for Tuesday night, then maybe Poole, Hull or White City on Wednesday, Thursday could be Sheffield or Ipswich, then either Hackney or Edinburgh on Friday then Belle Vue on Saturday… then it starts again." Sometimes, in months with a Bank Holiday in them, it could get even more hectic as Peter would squeeze in a Monday morning meet at King's Lynn. "I remember one time finishing late at a grass meet in Bielefeld on Sunday, driving to the ferry, crossing to the UK then up to King's Lynn for an 11am start. Legend has it I warmed the bike up in the back of the van on the way to the meet but I don't recall that. Though I did get changed as my friend was driving," he laughed. "Then we went from there to Hackney for the Monday evening."

The hectic lifestyle was a conscious decision by Peter, driven by the idea that the more he raced the better he'd get at it. This theory is borne out by other top-line ▶

▶

> *Legend has it I warmed the bike up in the back of the van on the way to the meet but I don't recall that. Though I did get changed as my friend was driving*

A HELPING HAND

At the start of his career Peter handled all his own maintenance, but by the time he was at the top of international racing even the best and most organised riders can't do everything themselves. Peter is keen to recognise all the help he received throughout his career. Jim Rowlinson was a key figure in the early days, then it was Guy Alcott who was prepping engines for Ivan Mauger and Ole Olsen at Belle Vue and offered to do the same for Peter when he joined the team. There was also a group of close friends who would drive bikes to meetings allowing him the chance to arrive later and fit in extra races. Later on, as a works rider for Weslake, he had Dave Nourish prepping engines for him, George Clarke accompanying him as mechanic and – for the world final in 1976 – the support of Eric Boocock.

n the start line for the Embassy Internationale at Wimbledon May 1978, Peter is in the yellow helmet cover.

competitors who all say that there is 'no substitute for practice.' Practice continued the year round, too, as when the UK season finished Peter was off to New Zealand or Australia to race there. It was this dedication – mixed with a healthy amount of natural skill – that would eventually pay off and see him top of the world.

WORLD CHAMPIONSHIP GLORY

Peter's world final record wasn't too bad for a young racer, and he'd already been in three finals when he arrived in Chorzów, Poland, for the final series in 1976. He remembered: "I was 12th in my first final which was in Poland in 1973, then in Gothenburg, Sweden, in 1974 I'd halved that to sixth. I felt I had a chance at Wembley for 1975 but the track wasn't in good condition. A crowd of 90,000 people were almost choked by dust because

Collins tucks in behind Michael Lee at the Wimbledon Internationale in 1978.

World Speedway Team Championships were another happy hunting ground for Peter. Here he slips underneath Australia's Phil Crump in the first round at Reading in 1978.

it hadn't been watered properly, someone somewhere managed to turn a hose on but all that happened was they flooded the track on the first bend. I'd won my first three races but in the fourth hit the water and went from first to last. I then met Ole Olsen in the final, and it was as good as over."

He'd begun the 1976 season by enjoying the winter season British Lions tour in Australia and New Zealand, but by March was back in the UK for the British season and the qualifying rounds for the individual world final. The rounds were at several venues around the country and went on through April and May with the big Intercontinental meeting at Wembley being the final qualifier.

By his own admission Peter felt he'd struggled during the qualifying rounds, and to compound matters the British final was at Coventry – the Midlands track not one of Collins's favourites – so he was delighted to finish fourth and secure his place at the Wembley final. Much more at home on the London track, and despite the stifling heat, Collins had a much better night – particularly when compared to reigning world champion Ole Olsen with the Dane falling foul of the referee and then suffering an engine failure that prevented him qualifying for the world final. Top of the pile on the night, Collins had left no one in any doubt he would be a contender for world success.

During this time he was also fulfilling his league race commitments – five nights a week – and also found time to take in the odd grass track such as the one billed as the Richest Ever Grass Track in Hereford. Of course, he won. ▶

SPONSORS

Being a good rider and a winner tends to attract sponsors and as well as being Weslake's top man, Peter enjoyed help from TT Leathers and Sportak, Daytona and initially Premier Helmets through Shane Hearty. That was until a visit to the Bell Helmets factory with Bruce Penhall brought about the connection with Bell. Oils were from Castrol and Elf while Renold supplied the chains and Henry Rosenthal provided Renthal handlebars. Dunlop kept rubber on the rear wheel.

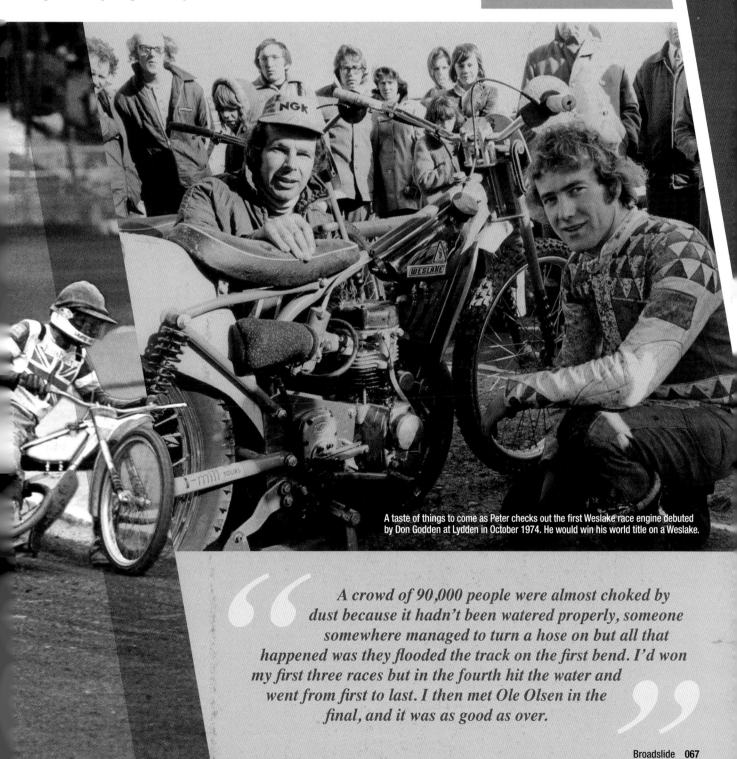

A taste of things to come as Peter checks out the first Weslake race engine debuted by Don Godden at Lydden in October 1974. He would win his world title on a Weslake.

> " A crowd of 90,000 people were almost choked by dust because it hadn't been watered properly, someone somewhere managed to turn a hose on but all that happened was they flooded the track on the first bend. I'd won my first three races but in the fourth hit the water and went from first to last. I then met Ole Olsen in the final, and it was as good as over. "

ABOVE: The comeback year for Peter after an accident ended his 1977 title defence, here he is on a Weslake at the European GP.

BELOW: Jawa-mounted for Ludlow grass track in 1975, it all helped to pay the bills.

BELOW: On the winning trail, Ludlow Grass Track in October 1974.

It was with this run of success behind him that he headed for Poland – the final due to take place on September 5. The BSPA – controlling body of the sport in the UK – chartered a plane to transport Collins, his fiancée Angela Hilton, Eric Boocock – so instrumental in keeping pressure off Peter and allowing the lad to concentrate on his racing – mechanic/friend George Clarke, Weslake's man Dave Nourish, and also along was Belle Vue promoter Jack Fearnley. They all flew out on Friday, practice was on Saturday and the racing was on Sunday in front of a crowd of 130,000.

"Speedway was a massive deal in those days," Peter said. "All the national daily papers had a speedway reporter and I even had a weekly column in the Daily Express." Things went well in practice, Peter even indulging in a little kidology by making mediocre turns near the pits but good ones out on the far side of the track. "I had two bikes with me; one was quite capable of winning the championship but the other was unbelievably good and this was the one that I used in the final." With his closest rival Ivan Mauger having dropped points, Peter just needed a second-place finish

to secure overall victory – and he remembered a tale about a racer in a previous world final who only needed to come third to win but was arrogantly rude to the other three riders in the race and finished fourth, losing his title by one point. Determined not to make a similar mistake, he said: "I kept out of Mauger's way on the track and while Ivan won the race, I was second across the line but world champion. And I was the first British champion since my hero Peter Craven in 1962, also an aces man." More than 40 years on, it's something that's still not sunk in.

The flight back to the UK was on Monday and Peter allowed himself a night off. "When we got home the whole village turned out to cheer me as 'their' world champion." The year wasn't over, either, and there was success of a different sort in November as Peter and Angela married.

A world champion he might have been, but at 22 his racing days were far from over and as title-holder his workload increased considerably and, as he recalled, everyone wanted a bit of him: "I even went to 10 Downing Street to meet Prime Minister Jim Callaghan! Then there were the races in Scandinavia and elsewhere in Europe, probably all the national fans wanted their top men to beat me but I thrived on that."

As he went into the 1977 series Peter felt he was riding better than in 1976. He'd carried on winning and even took part in the TV sporting superstars event, but unfortunately the year was marred by a freak accident which cost him the world championship. He'd set himself up for success by winning the Intercontinental final

again, and was mentally preparing himself for the world championship a fortnight later. Racing 'at home' on the Belle Vue track his hopes were shattered when he struck a drain cover – steel, two feet long and a foot wide – which flew up and clouted his leg. "The pain was unbelievable," he said grimacing. "I rolled to a halt and collapsed on the grass on the track. I knew it must be serious, but not how serious until I got to hospital. The cover had sliced through my leg to the bone and fractured the fibula; I was to be operated on that night and I remember telling Booey – Eric Boocock, team manager – 'don't let them put a cast on it, I've got to race next week in the final'. Surgeon Dr David Markham rebuilt my leg, and Jack Fearnley got permission for me to miss the official practice in Gothenburg a week later and flew me out to Sweden on the day of the final in a private jet. With Booey wheeling me round the track to see what the surface was like I was determined that if I was going to lose the title it would be racing, not sitting on the sidelines. I could hardly walk; a special boot had been made for me but I could still barely take the pain. A Swedish doctor examined me, read the letter from my surgeon and told me I was silly to ride. He signed me fit anyway." Hardly able to stand, Peter somehow finished second – only a point behind Mauger – but unfortunately 1976 would remain his only world championship success.

Various titles still came thick and fast until Peter's race career came to an end in 1986, however, and looking for an outlet for his spare energy he turned to restoration. He mostly concentrated on speedway machines,

but not exclusively – and his fitting and turning skills from his time with Shell came in handy again. He also bought a couple of vintage cars for weddings and grew this business to the point where five cars can be out at one time.

Pretty much retired now, Peter was very active until a brain haemorrhage laid him low. In typical Collins' determination, Peter refused to give up and has made a remarkable recovery. He now enjoys his time with his collection of speedway machines, and he owns one of every example of Weslake speedway bike including the five-valve which was banned before it ever raced. Visitors to such events as the Carole Nash International Classic MotorCycle show at Stafford will see Peter behind a stall with speedway bits and pieces on, enjoying chatting to racers, restorers and fans alike.

> ❝ *I rolled to a halt and collapsed on the grass on the track. I knew it must be serious, but not how serious until I got to hospital. The cover had sliced through my leg* ❞

CHAMPIONSHIPS AND ACHIEVEMENTS

Peter Collins has done a fair bit of winning in his racing life, the pinnacle being the world championship in 1976. Success had arrived before that, however, and it continued on after. Our list of his major successes barely does justice to the blood, sweat and anguish needed to achieve them so don't think of the glamour, think of the hundreds and thousands of miles travelling, the months away from home, frantic rebuilds during the night to get to the next meet and know Peter Collins earned every one of the results.

- **350CC GRASS TRACK CHAMPION: 1971, 1972**
- **WORLD TEAM CHAMPION: 1973, 1974, 1975, 1977, 1980.**
- **BRITISH LEAGUE CHAMPION: 1974, 1975**
- **EUROPEAN SPEEDWAY CHAMPION: 1974**
- **INTERCONTINENTAL CHAMPION: 1976, 1977**
- **WORLD INDIVIDUAL CHAMPION: 1976**
- **WORLD PAIRS CHAMPION: 1977 (WITH MALCOLM SIMMONS), 1980 (WITH DAVE JESSUP), 1983 (WITH KENNY CARTER), 1984 (WITH CHRIS MORTON)**
- **BRITISH SPEEDWAY CHAMPION: 1979**
- **137 ENGLAND CAPS**
- **ENGLAND AND BELLE VUE CAPTAIN**
- **AWARDED MBE FOR SERVICES TO MOTORCYCLING IN 2001**

The team man! Peter was one half of the Best Pairs grass track winners from May 1976.

LION-HEARTED

Wembley stadium has been home to many sports, and in the 1930s both the ice hockey and speedway teams used the Wembley Lions tag. It seemed an ideal opportunity to play on this and have a pair of lion cubs as mascots for the respective teams. So, a pair of nine-month-old cat kings were drafted on to the staff at Wembley and this photograph of them is their first official engagement. It's taken at Wembley in February 1937, and shows the members of Wembley Lions ice hockey team with speedway team captain Lionel Van Praag – who also brought his race machine along. It all looks very happy as the lads tickle the lion cubs behind the ears, but a couple of the expressions display wariness as to how big these cubs would grow before they were retired from modelling duties. Australian Van Praag was certainly 'lion-hearted' and won the Victoria Cross for heroism in the Second World War when he rescued the crew from his aeroplane when it ditched in the shark-infested waters of the Pacific Ocean.

Eso

It was a modern bike, but still with a separate oil tank. Oil in the frame was yet to come.

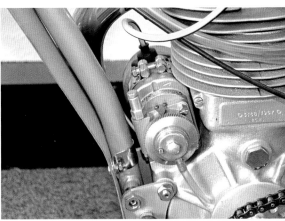

TOP LEFT CLOCKWISE: No protection or guards yet for the racer's primary drive.

ESO became Jawa after a takeover by the state.

A Lucas racing magneto provided the sparks, though by the time ESO was racing the magneto was becoming a thing of the past.

Clipped-on bars could move if the bike was dropped, therefore preventing damage.

When you're three-time world champion on one particular make of engine, then capture your fourth title on a completely different make of machine – and to cap it all off decide to set up as sole importer of said new machine – then the world had better take notice. And the world did take notice, because by 1968 the majority of the world's speedway riders were ESO-mounted, athough importer Barry Briggs was using the Jawa brand name.

The July 1968 issue of *The Motor Cycle* contained a feature on the Czech machine in which Briggo admitted the ESO engine power characteristics didn't suit every circuit, and acknowledged that reigning world champion Ove Fundin had decided to drop back to JAP power for the Wembley final. It was a decision ESO man Briggs agreed with as, apparently, Wembley was about the only circuit in the world that the JAP was right for. Briggo also added that when Fundin went to Belle Vue with the JAP, he was soundly beaten.

In further discussions with the reporter from *The Motor Cycle*, Barry added the ESO factory was much more familiar with the faster European tracks and this was why the motor was fitted with a Dellorto carburettor. In order to get some low-down punch for British tracks, Briggo just fitted an Amal GP. With

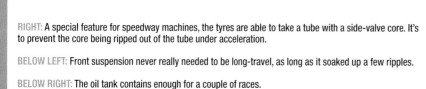

RIGHT: A special feature for speedway machines, the tyres are able to take a tube with a side-valve core. It's to prevent the core being ripped out of the tube under acceleration.

BELOW LEFT: Front suspension never really needed to be long-travel, as long as it soaked up a few ripples.

BELOW RIGHT: The oil tank contains enough for a couple of races.

A massive carb float bowl to hold the methanol is needed as these engines sup it like it's going out of fashion

this instrument in place the Czech motor is fine for all but the shortest of short tracks.

With the plain exhaust pipe, as fitted to the ESO in these pictures, the engine would give 54bhp when running on methanol, but on long tracks – with a reverse cone megaphone on the end – there's nearer 60bhp on tap. Add in power to 7000rpm, and safe to 8000rpm – with the rebuild gap as high as 30 meetings – and it's easy to see why the engine gained popularity fast.

In attempting to explain the reason behind the ESO's success, *The Motor Cycle* said the Czech motor had drawn on the basic concept of the JAP engine, that is to say they were both light, single-cylinder engines with pushrod valve operation, magneto ignition and total-loss oiling. Further inspection of the internals revealed a JAP-like inlet tract

with mild downdraught, a high-domed piston and spherical combustion chamber.

Where the ESO differs is in the bore and stroke; a much bigger bore and shorter stroke than the JAP gives freer breathing and higher revs when allied to a fierce cam with flat followers. Of course all this would be of little use if the bottom end flexed and floated around under pressure. Thankfully the ESO designers created a super-stiff base which accepts the longer barrel spigot to form a rigid barrel/crankcase join. Inside the cases is a crankshaft made up of two seven-inch x one-inch discs with one-inch diameter main shafts pressed in. These are located in caged roller

LEFT: Jawa lineage cutaway drawing.

bearings running in steel sleeves pressed into the alloy cases. For the big end the crank pin is a taper fit to the flywheels and the slots in the bearing cage house unequal rollers so a central wear ridge doesn't happen. This cage sits inside a steel con rod with extra stiffening around the big end eye and a light-alloy three-ring piston at the other end.

Four studs anchoring into bronze inserts hold the head and barrel in place and a range of shims and gaskets are available to adjust settings such as compression ratio and valve-spring length to their optimum settings. The timing train is well supported with an outrigger plate to prevent the cam spindles from flexing under pressure from the pushrods. This plate bolts to the spindles and the crank case, too.

In order to make maintenance easy, or at least speedy, there are several novel features such as detachable plugs to gain access to timing marks and tappet clearances.

So, the ESO/Jawa motor was all sweetness and light, but there was one cloud on the horizon. In common with all other similar motors there was a problem with dwindling magneto supplies. Lucas had stopped making them some time earlier in favour of more modern ignitions. The problem was a magneto was, and still is, a totally self-contained ignition unit with no need for wiring circuits, batteries and such things in order to make a spark happen at the right time in the right place. Way back in those days, Lucas had been cajoled into making a special batch of the magnetos for such engines as the ESO.

Once Barry Briggs got behind the ESO its profile rose considerably.

Oil is circulated via this pump, and the sight glasses in the top show how much is being fed.

LEFT: The rear hub is light and strong, but has no braking provision.

CLASSIC DIRTbike MAGAZINE

4 ISSUES FOR £15

Chapter 8

The 1930s: A decade of diversity

Dirt track racing was established as an attraction, now it was time for speedway to become a proper sport...

LEFT: Speedway was big business in the 1930s with stars flying in from all parts. This is a view of the Kings Oak track.

MAIN: At the start of the decade leg-trailers such as the Douglas ruled supreme.

The sport of dirt track was not fully formed when it arrived in the UK, but it was certainly a known concept and many of the major protagonists from Australia were familiar names to enthusiasts in Britain. Largely this was due to the writings of journalists in the motorcycle press of the day, journalists writing under such names as Ixion, Nitor and Talmage who were respected by the readers and the industry. Once word of this sport started to filter through to their ears, they picked up on the excitement of the whole thing and grasped almost immediately this was a spectacle. In particular Ixion – the Rev Basil H Davies – had produced a far-reaching article shortly after the High Beech meeting in which he highlighted the excitement of the dirt track when compared with other spectator-orientated sports. In his piece in *The Motor Cycle*

on May 17, 1928, Ixion suggested the appeal of dirt track was the intensity of the action: "…Go to Lords and you will drowse through hours of dull play. Go to Brooklands and the frightful speeds are camouflaged into insignificance by the vastness of the track. Go to a soccer league match and excitement is usually limited to a few flashes per game."

He went on to say how dirt track on a speedway was so short a race there was excitement continuously. This, he reckoned, would be the future of the sport for it appealed to the non-motoring enthusiast too.

As well as the interest in the riders and their techniques for broadsliding their machines at speed on the track, much speculation was given to the 'ideal' mount for this new phenomenon – and once again attention turned to the machines used in Australia. In almost every case these machines were owner-modified and helpfully *The Motor Cycle* detailed the modifications made to the AJS of Billy 'Monty' Lamont, the teenage superstar of dirt track in Australia. The

19-year-old Lamont recognised the need for a stiff frame and forks if only to keep the chain in line and prevent the forks from twisting. Another necessary fitting for the riders of the 1920s and 30s was the knee hook on the right-hand side. On entering a corner the rider would position himself so his knee would come under the hook and lock in position for the broadslide. With it being immediately obvious the dirt track rider would not spend much time with his left foot on a footrest, Lamont's machine didn't have one; should riders feel they needed such a fitting it was suggested it be mounted high up on the machine so it didn't catch in the ground on a turn and fetch the rider off. Though the knee hook has been consigned to history, other ideas used by Lamont are still around. He did, for instance, alter the frame so the engine was lower to the ground; he also abandoned gears in the gearbox, relying instead on a single ratio calculated to keep the ▶

England Wins the

ABOVE: You wouldn't mess with this lot would you? England's test match team from the 1931 test. They won.

LEFT: In a feature based on the question 'speedway – is it sport?', *The Motor Cycle's* Talmage illustrated intense rivalry by using this image of two riders battling it out.

BELOW: Australia's national squad parade before the UK crowd.

engine on the boil. With his modified equipment Lamont could lap at 55mph on a third-of-a-mile track, 65mph or more for a half-mile and he could top 80mph for a full mile-long track.

With public interest at a high and promoters keen to give it a go things looked rosy for this dirt track phenomenon, but world events outside of motorcycling were to play their part in changing the face of speedway. Speculation on the world's stock markets had been seen as a sure-fire way of making money and there were incredible amounts made by investors large and small throughout the 1920s. There were those who felt it couldn't last and several respected international financiers, speculators and investors urged caution as the signs of trouble rose. That they were proved correct in their attempts to warn of serious problems is a matter of financial rather than motorcycling history, but the record books show that on 'Black Tuesday' – 29 October 1929 – billions of dollars were wiped off share values on the American Stock Exchange in Wall Street and a 10-year Great Depression set in that affected all Western – and several non-Western – industrialised countries.

A NEED FOR GLAMOUR

Amid such a climate speedway was poised to

give the public some welcome glamour in austere times, and by and large it was a fair business as well with the controlling bodies resisting overtures from bookmakers to allow gambling at tracks. Some riders were elevated to the levels of modern-day footballer stardom, with earnings to match. There are stories of riders hiring aircraft to fly to meetings, others having teams of mechanics all paid for out of their winnings; speedway was truly a lucrative business.

One such acknowledged star was Jim Kempster, a Rudge rider who

allowed *The Motor Cycle* writer Talmage to describe his skills in a feature entitled The Dirttrack Art early in 1930. The feature showed how far English riders had progressed in the couple of years since dirt track was introduced to the country. It was notable for several reasons. The first was that it showed the sport was far more involved than just nailing the throttle wide open and hanging on. Second, the writer identified

sliding and broadsliding as two very different techniques – Talmage decided for the purpose of his feature in 1930 the term 'sliding' would refer to the normal method a speedway racer takes a corner with the handle bars on opposite lock, while 'broadsliding' would refer to a technique of both wheels sliding and the wheels in line. Third, and perhaps most significant, it contained the first reference to the sport being called speedway; yes, there are examples of dirt track riders described as racing on or at 'speedways', but *The Motor Cycle* issue of February 13,

1930, is the first mention of the dirt track racer being referred to as a 'speedway racer'.

Talmage also detailed the attraction of speedway, declaring that the non-motorcycling spectator was thrilled by the spectacle of motorcycles being slid around the track, by the excitement afforded by the occasional spill and by the cinders – of which the original tracks were made – being flung up at the corners. He also speculated that while the general public gave little thought to what was actually happening in front of them, the motorcycle enthusiast watching would have an understanding that they were seeing a controlled skid. The enthusiast would also know if they themselves were to hit a bend at speed on a loose surface then they too would skid and if they didn't – or couldn't – control it they would end in a heap.

Discussing the subject with one of the top racers in what was still a new sport, Talmage confirmed what he'd suspected: this new way of racing was a thinking man's (ladies had been banned, remember) arena and it seemed Jim Kempster was very good at thinking and transferring those thoughts to race-winning success. While Kempster allowed that all the thought in the world wouldn't be of any use if the rider hasn't the strength to hang on to the machine, the brains part of the required brains and brawn came well before it was time to race. The top competitor will study a schematic of the track, figure out the best way to get round the course, recall perhaps what gear ratio was used last time at the track and use that as his starting point. Once at the track he will study his fellow racers and watch where they go on the track so he can position himself correctly for the win.

But what of the machines doing the winning? There was much press speculation on machines which would be raising the cinder dust in the 1930s and it may seem odd to today's enthusiasts that the single-cylinder engine wasn't universally regarded as correct for the sport. In their review of the dirt track ▶

CIRCLE: Oops. Thrills AND spills were all part of the offering.

ABOVE: Squib Burton – star of British speedway – powers round Aussie Frank Arthur during the first test match of the year.

BELOW: What promoter wouldn't like to see that amount of people coming through the turnstiles? This is Stamford Bridge, circa 1931.

'inder Siftings

The tapes are up! Riders rocket forward, the crowd rise to cheer 'their' man on, you can almost smell the dope and 'R'...

ABOVE: Floodlit evening meetings attracted thousands.

BOTTOM: King of the Hill in 1931, nowhere in 1933... the demise of the Douglas.

machines on display at the Motorcycle Show in Olympia in the late 1920s there were singles from Sunbeam, Rudge and Blackburne, James supplied a V-Twin, Scott pinned its faith – as always – on a water-cooled two-stroke, and Douglas produced a newer version of its fore-and-aft twin. A marque absent from the list was one that would become synonymous with the sport, the JAP single. The London engine maker would not arrive in speedway until the 1931 season, and then only because racers such as Wal Phillips were friendly with people in the design department. Similarly, there was no uniform style to the speedway machine of the early 1930s – but it was on the horizon. Spectacular it might have been, but leg trailing was on the way out and the foot-forward sliding style was on the way in. Though the mainstay of the sport since its early days in Australia, the fore-and-aft Douglas was not to last as the top riders of the day realised the single-cylinder machine, with the engine low slung in a diamond frame, was the way forward.

The 1930s also witnessed the arrival of the start line-up that followers of speedway today would recognise. Rolling starts had been the norm since the sport came to the UK, but there were those riders who could play the field and by accelerating and decelerating on the approach make it seem as if the opposition were jumping the start. This was an offence punishable by exclusion and it took a canny official to spot it. Naturally this was deemed unsportsmanlike, but with high earnings available to winners such tricks were, if not commonplace, certainly known. The controlling authorities felt the way to remove this problem was to have a standing start. Factions within the sport were not happy, and didn't believe clutches would cope with the conditions, but along came Rudge to supply a bike with a version of its multi-plate TT clutch fitted to the countershaft. A top rider did 57 consecutive starts during a test day; the clutch needed no adjustment and it didn't even get hot. Point proved, National Speedway Association regulations met and so clutch starts were in. Of course, jumping the start would still be a punishable offence, but the onus would be on the individual rather than skulduggery by the opposition. Despite the grumbles from certain quarters when the season started, clutch starts were deemed successful and had enhanced the racing experience.

With early obstacles overcome and enhancements made, the sport was – in the words of the press – "here to stay". A national league was inaugurated in 1932 and organised along the lines of the

ABOVE: Thirsty work this dirt track lark.

BELOW: In the relatively early days of the moving picture, speedway provided a great spectacle.

football league with regular fixtures. Team riders were, if not household names, certainly well-known sporting personalities. There were also international test matches where national teams from various countries would compete in a series usually run in the visitors' off-season. Ergo the Aussies and Kiwis would come to the UK in our summer, the UK riders would head south in our winter. Things were looking good; the ACU had exerted a degree of control over the scene, the tracks with poor administration had folded and the bikes had developed to the point where speedway – as it's recognised today – was practised on nights all over the country. Unfortunately, however, world events would once again come into play at the end of the decade when in 1939 a second major conflict of the century engulfed the globe.

The motorcycle press tried to keep the interest up and the *The Motor Cycle's* man, writing almost exactly a month after war was declared in the UK, featured a piece describing what it was like to be in the saddle of a speedway machine. His subject was Wimbledon's top man Lionel Van Praag who showed Talmage a thing or two. The writer described how alien the concept of riding a speedway bike was to a road rider: "Imagine reaching to pick up a petrol tin (one of those old-fashioned steel two-gallon ones) and instead of it being full it's almost empty, such is the feeling of a speedway machine to a roadster." With 40bhp on tap and all it has to haul is a bike less than the weight of a smaller two-stroke,

ABOVE: A crossover point in styles, leg trailing was the traditional method but the foot-forward style was increasing.

BELOW: Close racing was the key to big crowds. People wanted excitement, not a procession.

Talmage found the experience to be exhilarating. Handling was pin-point-perfect, acceleration phenomenal and woe betide anyone who shuts off in the corner as he will be pitched over the top. No, what one must do is open the throttle judiciously and make the rear wheel slide – any ham-fistedness will result in it all going wrong. Delay too long in opening the throttle and the front end is lost, get on it too soon and everyone passes you. Talmage concluded: "So, now you can go ride a speedway machine… all you need is years of practice."

THE MODERN SPEEDWAY MOUNT

In *The Motor Cycle* dated February 2, 1933, there was a picture indicating the speedway world had changed and what could be easily recognised as the first modern dirt track machine was presented in all its glory. The JAP speedway model had actually been thought about, and the peculiar requirements of the speedway world had been met. With its rigid, diamond frame, Webb dirt track forks, underslung fuel tank and the engine as a stressed member holding the lot together, this was the way the sport would progress. Why did JAP use a Rudge frame? Simply because its own version was too rigid and the Rudge offered a degree of flexibility which riders preferred – the feeling was a stiff frame would pitch the machine straight when whacking open the throttle in a turn. External engine modifications for the new JAP single included angling the carburettor away from the flying cinders, shale or dirt, while inside a stiffer big-end and longer con rod were expected to cure breakages in this area. A double delivery oil pump forced oil to everywhere it should.

CURRENT CHAT

NO FOOLING HERE

There are certain sportsmen whose names transcend their own sphere and become known to the nation as a whole, even if those hearing it are not fans of their sport. Such a name is Barry Briggs, and he seems to have been part of the speedway scene forever and a day – and at the top in three of those decades. When this photograph was taken on April 1, 1958, Briggo was the reigning world champion and great things were expected of him and his Wimbledon team-mate Cyril Brine for the coming season.

The first meeting of that year was scheduled to be a few days later on April 4 when the Manchester team would travel down to London for the Good Friday races. Manchester's top man, Peter Craven, was noted as a superb rider with his own distinctive style, a precursor to the modern lay-down style almost, and the duel with Kiwi Briggo was expected to be an early season highlight of the British Match Race series.

Godden GR500

This is what can happen when a talented engineer and dedicated racer is
unhappy with the then current crop of racers… he makes his own.

TOP LEFT CLOCKWISE: Noise concerns on tracks in city centres led to the introduction of silencers. There is the added benefit of being able to tune power with a silencer, too.

GTS? GTS stands for Gerry T Smith and one of the few non-Godden bits.

Now, let's see, who made this magnesium spool hub? Yes, you've got it… Godden. With no need for brakes the hub is very simple.

The oiling system is quite simple.

A talented racer, engineer and businessman all wrapped up in a package called Don Godden. Don began making his own frames in the 1960s with his own ideas incorporated in their design, and initially with JAP engines fitted. By 1970 he was established enough as a frame maker to start Godden Engineering. A collaboration with Harry Weslake led to Don developing its race engine, but in pushrod form with double the normal number of valves in the head. The engine was successful and Godden was one of two distributors of the product, which fitted in well with his frame, gearbox, wheel, fork and other accessories already on his books. A change in policy at Weslake led to Godden designing the GR500 – Godden Racing 500 – launched in 1979; the launch feature was published in *The Motor Cycle* during January 1979 and is reprinted elsewhere in this publication with full details. In basic terms, putting the camshaft upstairs so it could operate the four valves directly with no bendy pushrods to interfere with the cam timing gives a superbly reliable race engine which maintains its power delivery throughout the race.

By the time this 1985 Godden was produced the marque was well known and ▶

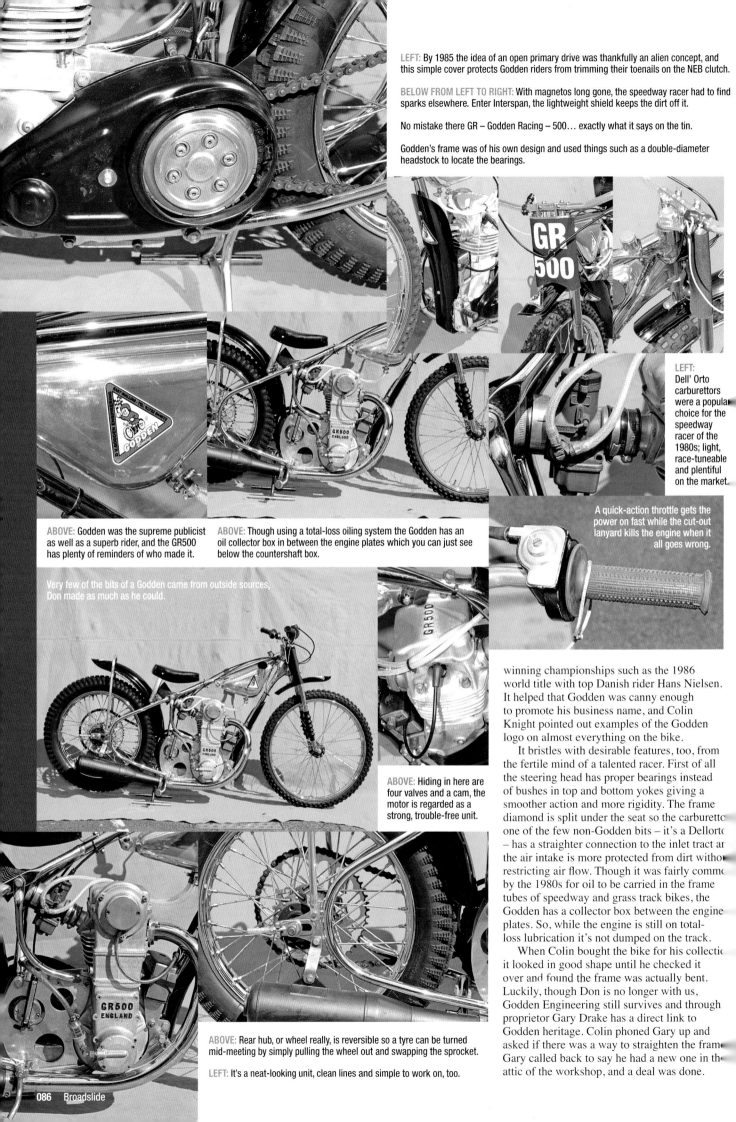

LEFT: By 1985 the idea of an open primary drive was thankfully an alien concept, and this simple cover protects Godden riders from trimming their toenails on the NEB clutch.

BELOW FROM LEFT TO RIGHT: With magnetos long gone, the speedway racer had to find sparks elsewhere. Enter Interspan, the lightweight shield keeps the dirt off it.

No mistake there GR – Godden Racing – 500… exactly what it says on the tin.

Godden's frame was of his own design and used things such as a double-diameter headstock to locate the bearings.

LEFT: Dell' Orto carburettors were a popular choice for the speedway racer of the 1980s; light, race-tuneable and plentiful on the market.

A quick-action throttle gets the power on fast while the cut-out lanyard kills the engine when it all goes wrong.

ABOVE: Godden was the supreme publicist as well as a superb rider, and the GR500 has plenty of reminders of who made it.

ABOVE: Though using a total-loss oiling system the Godden has an oil collector box in between the engine plates which you can just see below the countershaft box.

Very few of the bits of a Godden came from outside sources, Don made as much as he could.

ABOVE: Hiding in here are four valves and a cam, the motor is regarded as a strong, trouble-free unit.

ABOVE: Rear hub, or wheel really, is reversible so a tyre can be turned mid-meeting by simply pulling the wheel out and swapping the sprocket.

LEFT: It's a neat-looking unit, clean lines and simple to work on, too.

winning championships such as the 1986 world title with top Danish rider Hans Nielsen. It helped that Godden was canny enough to promote his business name, and Colin Knight pointed out examples of the Godden logo on almost everything on the bike.

It bristles with desirable features, too, from the fertile mind of a talented racer. First of all the steering head has proper bearings instead of bushes in top and bottom yokes giving a smoother action and more rigidity. The frame diamond is split under the seat so the carburetto one of the few non-Godden bits – it's a Dellorto – has a straighter connection to the inlet tract ar the air intake is more protected from dirt witho restricting air flow. Though it was fairly comm by the 1980s for oil to be carried in the frame tubes of speedway and grass track bikes, the Godden has a collector box between the engine plates. So, while the engine is still on total-loss lubrication it's not dumped on the track.

When Colin bought the bike for his collecti it looked in good shape until he checked it over and found the frame was actually bent. Luckily, though Don is no longer with us, Godden Engineering still survives and through proprietor Gary Drake has a direct link to Godden heritage. Colin phoned Gary up and asked if there was a way to straighten the fram Gary called back to say he had a new one in th attic of the workshop, and a deal was done.

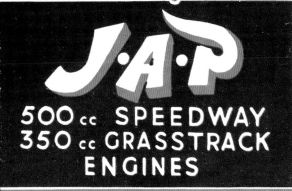

Chapter 9

The 1940s: The dark days

The onset of the Second World War halted speedway's progress, so attention turned to reflecting on its formative years and how the sport could be improved once it resumed...

Wembley's Tommy Price was the first post-Second World War British Speedway champion.

Fuel for private use became a scarce commodity during and after the Second World War, and so the sporting world was on hold for most of the 1940s. The motorcycle press was doing its bit to bolster morale by reminding readers of what had been, what had been expected and what might be once hostilities were over and the world returned to normal. There were teams that continued to race with official permission during the Second World War, with Belle Vue – under the control of Alice Hart – being one who kept meetings alive during this troubled time. With petrol increasingly restricted for anything but the most essential requirements, the programmes from those wartime meetings proudly announced 'No Petrol Whatsoever Is Used.' The fuel used was methanol, a wood alcohol concoction produced by using acids on items that contain cellulose – such as wood (the reality is a lot more complicated than the brief description suggests), but the fact of the matter was that it allowed racing to continue. The riders for these meetings came from servicemen on leave, or those who could get time off from reserved occupations. Undoubtedly the continuation of racing at Belle Vue during the Second World War contributed to their winning the national trophies in 1946 and 1947.

While this publication is concerned primarily with the history of speedway, nothing happens in a vacuum and some context has to be placed on what's being described and why things happened in certain ways. Rationing loomed large over wartime life, and all sorts of things were restricted as the years went on; fuel obviously, but paper was also on the list and that affected the press. It meant regular copies of *The Motor Cycle* and *Motor Cycling* would be reduced in size and paper quality. The lack of sport to reflect on was clear, and features were based around what had been happening in speedway and snippets of news about racers now in the forces. Lionel Van Praag, captain of Wimbledon and then in the Royal Australian Air Force, was one such example; the story of how he had won the George Medal when rescuing his crew after his plane crashed into shark-infested waters of the Pacific certainly stands out. ▶

Earlier in the conflict however, particularly in the initial eight-month period where there were no major military land operations on the Western Front, there had been an attempt to 'carry on as normal' and as a result *The Motor Cycle* of March 1940 contained a short piece in which Talmage proclaimed 'Speedway Racing Again'; and it continued to reflect on the first race meets of the year at West Ham and Belle Vue. There were some differences – fuel had been immediately restricted – and so the low octane 'pool' petrol was all that was available. It didn't seem to matter, with near 15,000 packing into West Ham and a further programme of Saturday afternoon racing was planned. Sadly the initial 'Phoney War' was just a time of consolidation, and when action began in earnest race meets took a back seat. While events

were licensed for some holiday weekends at several venues, the press had to contend with soul-stirring features on exploits of the past.

Researching through more than 600 wartime back issues of *The Motor Cycle* and *Motor Cycling* showed lots of things were on the backburner during this period, and page fillers were frequent. Two reasonable-sized features did leap out, however, and the first saw racer Wal Phillips describe his debut speedway meeting in the late 1920s, and what a description it was.

WAL PHILLIPS

Phillips provided a fascinating insight into a world where a lad could ride a motorcycle to a speedway meet, take part in the racing and even challenge for the win.

He started the piece by saying he arrived at Stamford Bridge well before any racing was to be done, his only preparation at the track amounted to removing his JAP-Scott's headlight after which he and his friend Jack "wandered off for a cup of tea." Phillips stated he wasn't the least bit nervous as he'd no thoughts of winning the event and was treating it more as a practice session for which he'd paid seven shillings and sixpence for the privilege. He was so unconcerned with success he'd not even removed the mudguards or silencer from his machine, nor did he worry much about warming it up as it was so worn it made little difference hot or cold.

By the start of the meeting Phillips was all fired up and the grand parade of riders, which started off as a gentle ride to introduce them

TWENTY YEARS AN ACE

What was the secret of a 42-year-old racer remaining at the top of his speedway profession when many contemporaries had long since retired? That was the question *The Motor Cycle* asked race-ace Jack Parker. In a two-page interview the magazine learned Parker was first, last and always a motorcyclist, as keen on the sport in his 40s as he had been in his 20s. Parker also admitted he knew his limitations and this allowed him to remain competitive at his advanced age – 42 at the time of the feature in 1948. One of the dirt track pioneers, Parker raced seven meetings in one week, including an

afternoon race at High Beech followed by a frantic dash to Leicester for the evening race during which he covered 2000 miles by road. The effect of the non-stop workload on his body was phenomenal – losing two stone in body weight – and realised if he didn't pace himself he'd not last. He was virtually teetotal, insisted on regular meals and the proper quota of sleep and rather than go hell-for-leather in every race Parker restricted such attempts to where it really was needed – probably the first racer to implement such a professional regime to his endeavours. To keep his brain active, Parker was interested in the design of his machines – and he believed being 'switched on' helped when

promoters struggled with basic addition on calculating payouts. The fact he understood weight distribution, rather than simply 'weight' often made a winning difference, and he was smart enough to allow for the fact that the equations were different for every rider. It also meant the constant search for ultimate power was not always a good thing in his eyes; what he wanted instead was the right power in the right place. Parker's home track at Belle Vue had employed an engineer and a dynamometer to find out just how engines were performing, and it was observed that what made a good dyno engine wasn't always a good track engine.

Few new machines were available postwar so older bikes were
pressed into action… and that meant older styles, too.

to the crowd, turned into an impromptu race during which the marshals struggled to retain order. Once they did, and the riders headed to the pits, he recalled that the enormity of what he was about to do kicked in. There were enough people in the stands to rival a football cup semi-final crowd, and suddenly Wal was nervous wondering how he would feel if they booed or hooted at him? Then in the programme was Gus Kuhn, a racer Wal had met and been beaten by at a non-speedway race at Crystal Palace.

Wal went into his 'race zone' – the crowd and other riders ignored – concentrating solely on the starter. Time slowed as the starter's finger twitched, then the gun went off and so did Phillips! One lap, then two; in his mind he was thinking about winning until Gus Kuhn flashed past miles-an-hour faster. Kuhn pitched into the next turn, Phillips held the throttle wide and caught him, Kuhn pulled away on the straight, Phillips caught him again at the turn and again Kuhn pulled away on the straights. Above the noise of his machine Phillips heard a dull roar and thought perhaps his mount was on the way out, so backed off slightly to allow Kuhn the win. In the pits his machine sounded perfect. The next race was the same – the dull roar again – but Phillips pushed on. Wal said: "I took appalling risks on the turns in an effort to stay in front, time and time again I slid wildly past him only to be overhauled on the straights." For his final race of the evening Phillips was determined to remain flat out and he hit the first bend and went into the closest thing to a broadslide he'd managed all evening. The bumpy track was pitching the bike this way and that, and still Kuhn overhauled him. Phillips asked the question "perhaps if I followed him?" but ended with a face full of cinders from the rear wheel of his rival. Still going flat out he moved to the outside of the track and managed to pass his rival and was leading to the line… 10 yards… five yards… damn! Kuhn on the line by a wheel! With the adrenalin easing off, Phillips noticed the dull roar again; it was the crowd shouting his name. His antics trying to beat Kuhn had caused a commotion and they wanted to see him back on the track. The races went on and the crowd roared Phillips' name over and over until the promoter, one Claude Langdon, rushed red-faced into the pits, waving his arms and yelling at Phillips to go out and do a demo race on his own. "How much?" queried Phillips. Langdon apparently went an even deeper shade of red at the audacity of this unknown rider.

Phillips went out on the track, did a few laps as fast as he could, fell a lot, and the crowd loved him the more for it. Back in the pits stood Langdon, with the news he'd arranged a match race with Doug Wilson at the end of the meeting, after which Phillips was to head to the Royal Box to be presented with a cheque by Kaye Don – the noted pre-First World War racing driver. The match race was as close as his earlier ones had been, but this time the result went in Phillips's favour by a few inches.

An envelope was handed over, Phillips took the adulation of the crowd and tried to make his way back to the pits – 50 yards took 15 minutes as men slapped his back and women hugged him. He reached the sanctuary of the pits and ripped open the envelope to find a sheet ▶

> *I took appalling risks on the turns in an effort to stay in front, time and time again I slid wildly past him only to be overhauled on the straights.*

of white paper! Later though he received a cheque for £12 10s – more money than he'd ever had in his life.

This edited summary of Wal's first speedway meet is almost as thrilling as the full-length one, and even allowing for his own spin on things it is – according to the reporter who was at that first meet – quite an accurate retelling. It seems Phillips was a bit of a showman, and with the ability to back it up. Sometime later in his career as a speedway racer Phillips attempted to break the Stamford Bridge track record during a meeting. Though races had by then become four laps, Phillips reasoned if he did a five-lap race he could tackle two records at once – they being the standing start one using the first four laps and the flying start using the last four laps.

Again Phillips used his 'never shut off' technique and hurled his Douglas around like a madman. Twice he clipped the wooden fencing as the bike hurtled round the track. For the fifth lap he was beginning to tire and elected to ease off slightly as he felt too exhausted to hold on and hitting the fence once more might put him in the crowd – probably not enamouring himself to those he landed on. Still, he hung on and crossed the line and slowed rapidly on his way to the pits where he heard the announcer tell the crowd "Wal Phillips has set new lap records for Stamford Bridge."

THE FUTURE OF SPEEDWAY
As the 1940s went on and Allied victory in the Second World War became more and more likely, thoughts turned to the resumption of full-scale sport in the UK, including speedway. In December 1944, *The Motor Cycle* got the opinions of eight well-known promoters: Mr AJ Elvin, managing director of Wembley Stadium; Mr EO Spence in charge at Belle Vue stadium; Fred Mockford at New Cross; Victor Martin who'd just relinquished co-control of West Ham in favour of his own speedway manufacturing company; Mr RW Greene MBE who was promoter at Wimbledon; ACU secretary TW Loughborough; Kenneth Duthie who was secretary of the speedway riders association; and the legendary Johnnie Hoskins.

Questions aimed at these venerable gentlemen were apparently the ones which enthusiasts were wanting to know. For instance speedway fans were concerned to know how soon speedway would begin again after the war ended? Would there be training facilities for the encouragement of new riders? What was the likelihood of new tracks emerging? What would the controlling rules of the sport be – as before or new? Would tracks see the emergence of supercharged multi-cylinder machines with speeds far in excess of what had gone before? In the feature built around the replies, *The Motor Cycle* felt it had skimmed the cream of the information and was confident of the accuracy of the report.

Addressing the 'how soon?' question, Elvin suggested that if the hostilities ended in spring then racing could start in the summer of 1945. He also considered that racing could start at Wembley as there was enough equipment available. A stumbling block though could be entertainment tax, levied at 43% of the gate.

Looking from a manufacturer's point of view, Martin was also of the opinion speedway would start sooner rather than later in 1945 and the required ancillary components were available or their supply chain secured

as early as December 1944. Martin's only issue was with new tyres, and he was confident this would resolve itself – as would the fuel situation. Other estimations of the restart of racing included Mockford's who reckoned it would be four weeks; Greene said "summer at the latest."

Regarding training of new riders there was a considerable amount of agreement about the need to provide facilities, but an equal amount of difference in what form it should take. For one – Wembley – it involved leasing a complete track and appointing a trainer; for others – Belle Vue and New Cross – it was more facilities at their own tracks; at Wimbledon the theory was 'bring your bike and have a go'; Hoskins' view was against providing training facilities as "the lads we want in speedway are the ones who are keen enough to make the initial efforts themselves."

Once on the subject of machinery, all were in basic agreement that the motorcycles at the restart of speedway would reflect what was being raced in 1939 – but the opinions differed from there. One suggested multi-cylinders and supercharging, another suggested 350cc motors, the ACU man suggested no interference in the design but perhaps a capacity limit. Interestingly, a couple thought that the Government's spending on engine power research ought to be tapped into in the interests of reliability; and perhaps a bit of standardisation should be enforced as it was felt the spectacle was provided by the riders rather than the machines.

Just pop on that racer, Harry, old chap. No need to worry about a helmet here, lad…

ABOVE: A post-Second World War test match, British Lions against the Australian Kangaroos.

RIGHT: Wal Phillips's speedway mount. Phillips being Phillips, this was different to the rest, but still worked better.

A TALE OF TWO MACHINES

By 1948 Wal Phillips's racing days were over, but the charismatic fellow had taken on managing the Harringay Speedway team where he supervised preparation of the team machines and experimented with various ideas of his own. At the end of the season he invited *The Motor Cycle's* Harry Louis along to try Harringay's star man Vic Duggan's machine, and then one that had been 'subjected' to a few of Wal's theories. At the track Harry was instructed to drop the clutch on Duggan's machine and ease in the throttle very slowly. Louis was grateful for the long expanse of concrete at Harringay arena as he teetered away on the championship-winning machine. The slightest blip of the twistgrip had the front wheel pawing the air and the journalist found it both exhilarating and disconcerting for the power to come in so early. Unlike road racers where the power comes in at 4000-5000rpm the speedway machine was producing power at just 400-500rpm. With only the barest of protective clothing and not even a helmet, Louis set off for the practice section of the arena in the company of Phillips and his special horizontal engine machine. "Just put your left foot forward, cant the bike over slightly and turn it up," the past master instructed, loudly. To his own surprise Harry found himself sliding, and reasonably well. With more practice he went even better, right up until he was too confident and fell to earth. Expecting a row for dropping the team's star machine an hour or so before a meeting Louis was surprised to have his spill laughed off with the comment '…pretty much crash-proof, just shake out the cinders and off you go again…'
In his chats with Phillips, the writer learned speedway racers fight a constant battle against wheelspin while trying to get as much traction as possible. The technique in that postwar period was foot forward rather than the old-fashioned leg-trailing style seen 20 years earlier, and Harry found the low-down weight of the bike to help in controllability. It's no surprise then that he felt much more secure on Wal Phillips's personal machine, with its all but horizontal engine. Louis reminded readers of Phillips's early Scott-based machines where his engine was canted well forward and able to out-handle faster

machines. So it seemed was the case with this 1948 creation which proved remarkably fast in the hands of team-man Jimmy Grant who claimed to be okay but not a top-liner. In true journalistic style, Louis wanted to know what was inside and, expecting cagey answers alluding to wild cams and high compression, was surprised to find Phillips remarkably frank about the state of tune. Wal revealed that he'd been at the JAP works and spent time experimenting with the speedway engine. He found that while it was possible to make the engine produce more power, it was completely wrong for speedway. What was needed for success was the low-down torque of the engine's power delivery, and hence there was nothing special about the engines under Phillips's care.

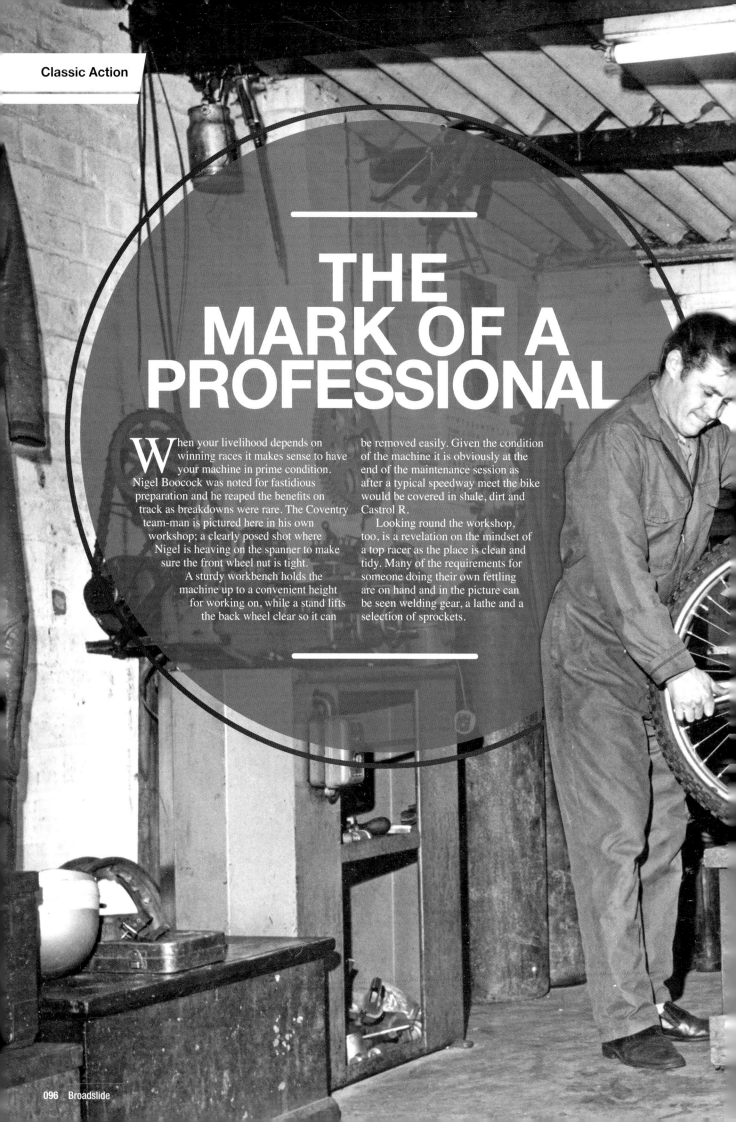

THE MARK OF A PROFESSIONAL

When your livelihood depends on winning races it makes sense to have your machine in prime condition. Nigel Boocock was noted for fastidious preparation and he reaped the benefits on track as breakdowns were rare. The Coventry team-man is pictured here in his own workshop; a clearly posed shot where Nigel is heaving on the spanner to make sure the front wheel nut is tight.

A sturdy workbench holds the machine up to a convenient height for working on, while a stand lifts the back wheel clear so it can be removed easily. Given the condition of the machine it is obviously at the end of the maintenance session as after a typical speedway meet the bike would be covered in shale, dirt and Castrol R.

Looking round the workshop, too, is a revelation on the mindset of a top racer as the place is clean and tidy. Many of the requirements for someone doing their own fettling are on hand and in the picture can be seen welding gear, a lathe and a selection of sprockets.

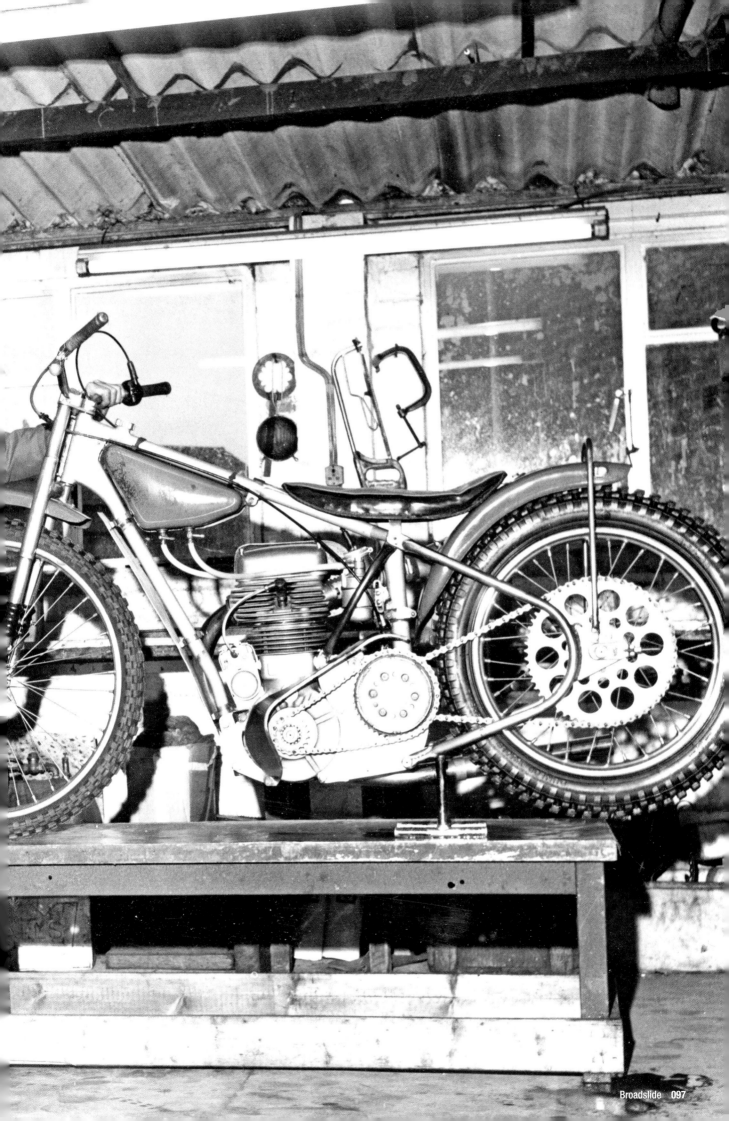

Dirt track Douglas

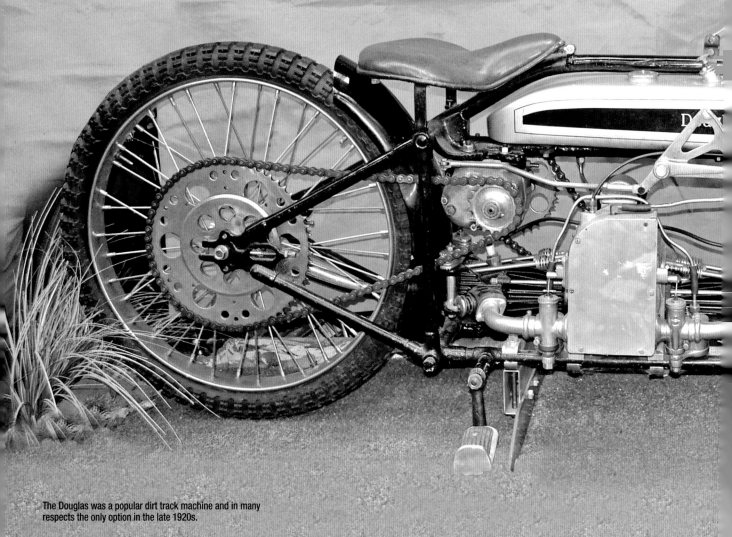

The Douglas was a popular dirt track machine and in many respects the only option in the late 1920s.

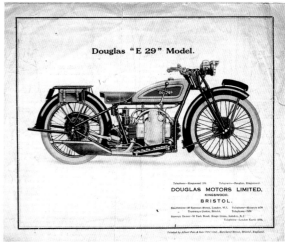

Douglas "E 29" Model.

DOUGLAS MOTORS LIMITED,
KINGSWOOD,
BRISTOL.

Douglas Separate Unit Electric Lighting.

After many years experimenting with electric lighting systems of all kinds, the outfit illustrated has been found to give complete satisfaction.

It is of the separate unit type as used in modern car practice and incorporates a separate permanent field generator driven through a shock absorbing device, a sealed cut out and a powerful head lamp controlled by a switch at the back of the lamp, easily accessible to the rider and gives the following positions:—

"On; charge; full; dim."

The resistance is incorporated in the switch to prevent damage to the battery by the passing of excessive current. The battery is carried in a convenient position on the saddle tube in an enclosed metal case.

The generator and cut out are built to Douglas design by Messrs. B.T.H. Ltd., and can be relied upon to give good service without maintenance troubles.

It is a distinct advantage over other sets employing a combined magneto and generator, and its universal adoption by the motor car industry is concrete proof that our principle is correct.

PRICE - Solo   £6 : 5 : 0
(Head and Tail)

Combination   £6 : 15 : 0
(Head, Tail and Side)

BEWARE!

There are a great number of spare parts for DOUGLAS machines that are not of our manufacture being offered to the public. These should be avoided, as they are likely to cause trouble. Even those sold as W.D. Spares may not be genuine DOUGLAS manufacture, and are probably of very inferior quality.

If you risk fitting these to your machine you will probably be let down sooner or later with a badly smashed engine, which in the end will cost you far more than the price of the genuine DOUGLAS part.

Douglas

SPARES

TRADE   D   MARK

BUY ONLY GENUINE DOUGLAS SPARES

SIDECARS.

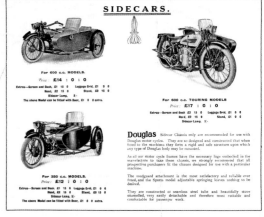

For 600 c.c. MODELS.
Price : £14 : 0 : 0
Extras—Screen and Dash, £1 10 0   Luggage Grid, £1 0 0
Hood, £2 15 0   Stand, £0 15 0
Sidecar Lamp, 5/-
The above Model can be fitted with Door, £1 0 0 extra.

For 600 c.c. TOURING MODELS
Price : £17 : 0 : 0
Extras—Screen and Dash £3 15 0   Luggage Grid, £1 0 0
Hood, £2 15 0   Stand, £1 0 0
Sidecar Lamp, 5/-

For 350 c.c. MODELS.
Price : £12 : 0 : 0
Extras—Screen and Dash, £1 15 0   Luggage Grid, £1 0 0
Hood, £2 15 0   Stand, £0 15 0
Sidecar Lamp, 5/-
The above Model can be fitted with Door, £1 0 0 extra.

Douglas Sidecar Chassis only are recommended for use with Douglas motor cycles. They are so designed and constructed that when fitted to the machines they form a rigid and safe structure upon which any type of Douglas body may be mounted.

As all our motor cycle frames have the necessary lugs embodied in the manufacture to take these chassis, we strongly recommend that all prospective purchasers fit the chassis designed for use with a particular machine.

The mudguard attachment is the most satisfactory and reliable ever fitted, and the Sports model adjustable springing leaves nothing to be desired.

They are constructed of seamless steel tube and beautifully stove enamelled, very easily detachable and therefore most suitable and comfortable for passenger work.

ABOVE: Douglas, dirt track pioneers.

In the beginning of certainly the UK's involvement with dirt track, competitors rode what they had. There were instantly recognised requirements for a dirt tracker and right from the start those early racers were stripped of equipment such as mudguards, lights and one footrest. As the scene progressed rapidly brakes were ditched and smaller fuel tanks made to hold enough fuel for one race. Manufacturers cottoned on to this scene and by November 1928, eight months after the High Beech meeting, no less than 17 major manufacturers had specialised dirt track models on display at the Olympia show in London. *The Motor Cycle's* man, Talmage, feted the Douglas as being the top performer in the fledgling sport.

The company was almost ideally placed to take advantage of the dirt track requirements with a minimalist version of its TT racer. By the late 1920s the Douglas TT machine was looking a little dated on the road race scene, but performed well on the dirt. It had the advantage of an engine design which kept the weight as low down as possible, a reasonably long wheelbase and a power output which was both spread across the rev range and produced reliably. With no actual engine size stated for dirt track – though convention seemed to settle on 500cc as that was the capacity of most performance-orientated singles from the British industry – Douglas produced the Dirt Track model in two capacities, 500 and 600cc. Power output from the 500cc engine was claimed at 27bhp but it was possible to

LEFT: The carburettor breathes in an airbox which was unusual for the time.

BELOW: A gauze sheet allows the cooling air, such as it could be on a speedway track, to flow over the front cylinder while keeping dirt off the engine.

ABOVE: Once into top gear, the gear change lever was redundant.

RIGHT: It doesn't actually pay to ponder on what would happen to various bits of a rider should the chains let go…

A little bit of springing and a little bit of damping was all that was needed in those days.

Douglas "A.29." 3.5 h.p.
Side Valve.

Douglas "B.29." 3.5 h.p.
Side Valve.

Douglas "D.29." 3.5 h.p.
O.H.V. Sports.

Douglas "E.29." 5.9 h.p.
Side Valve.

Douglas "F.29." 5.9 h.p.
Side Valve.

Douglas "G.29." 5.9 h.p.
O.H.V.

Douglas "H.29." 5.9 h.p.
O.H.V.

SPECIAL NOTES.

Douglas T.T. Model.
494 c.c. O.H.V.

Dirt Track Model.
494 c.c. O.H.V.

ABOVE: Douglas even catalogued a dirt track bike.

have a factory-tuned engine for a further tenner which hopped the power up to 32bhp. There were even super-tuned options apparently available as the noted Douglas tuner of the day – Bert Dixon – could persuade the horizontally opposed twins to produce 34.5bhp. The search for power was a two-way thing as the factory frequently checked over the engines of top riders to see what was wearing and what was not.

For most of 1928 and 1929 Douglas pretty much had it all to itself, sales were excellent with one promoter of speedway ordering 50 machines, and at shows the Douglas stand was a meeting point for top riders. Sadly for Douglas it was not to last and the new decade brought more serious challenges from Rudge and a breed of specials using JAP engines. Sales declined, a price cut from £85 for the 500 and £90 for the 600 to £75 for either had little effect and by 1933 the Dirt Track Douglas machines – lauded as 'the winners of thousands of races' – were gone from the range.

OCTOBER 26-29 2017

STONELEIGH PARK
WARWICKSHIRE CV8 2LZ

DIRT BIKE SHOW

IN PARTNERSHIP WITH

MOTUL

THE *LATEST 2018 BIKES* FROM ALL MAJOR MANUFACTURERS

EUROPE'S LARGEST OFF-ROAD EVENT

100S OF TRADE AND RETAIL STANDS TO *BAG A BARGAIN*

THRILLING LIVE ACTION

FUN FOR THE *WHOLE FAMILY*

MEET AND GREET *OFF ROAD STARS*

ADVANCE TICKETS ON SALE NOW!

❮ Tickets starting from £8
❮ Under 10s go FREE

NEW & IMPROVED

TICKET HOTLINE: 01507 529529 \ Trade: 01507 529594

WWW.DIRTBIKESHOW.CO.UK

Chapter 10

The 1950s: A time of great change

The halcyon era of the 1930s was a dim and distant memory in the 1950s, and there were those that believed the glory days of speedway were well and truly over…

As the 1950s dawned there seemed to be a change in the way speedway was reported. Yes, there were still some news items in the two major motorcycle publications but not nearly as many as there had been in the 1930s. It almost seemed as though speedway was becoming a subculture and tending to polarise opinions. Features did still appear, and in June 1951 an intriguing technical feature appeared in *The Motor Cycle* with Australian George 'Snowy' Rogers as its subject. The lad had made a name for himself in the early dirt track scene in the 1920s and such was his reputation for fixing stuff that he was tasked with looking after 'Sprouts' Elder's machinery when the American hill climb champion went to Australia to try this dirt track thing. Elder was successful so headed for the UK scene, but Rogers had so much work on he couldn't leave Australia.

He did finally make it to the UK in 1949, assessed what was happening on the smaller tracks used here and developed a few ideas of his own; one in particular caught the writer's eye. Rogers reckoned when the typical speedway machine was sliding into an anti-clockwise turn – banked over to the left with the rear wheel sliding to the right and the steering turned to the right to counteract the slide – the front wheel wanted to push out to the right, too. The more it drifted the more lock was needed and the more the back wheel came around. Rogers felt if the front wheel centre could be kept in line with the frame, regardless of the lock, then there would be more traction, more speed and greater safety.

So, with the idea in his head, Rogers set to and came up with his unique idea which he patented. In brief detail, the fork yokes are able to move in the steering head so they allow the fork-centre to be always in line with the frame centre. Steering lock is restricted to 45 degrees, but most riders use less than 25 degrees lock in a race anyway, and if they go higher it's the beginning of over-slide and likely to end in a heap. To counteract this Rogers also invented a throttle device which automatically backed off the power allowing the rider to save the spill and when the lock returned to normal the full cable action was returned. How did this happen? Rogers created a device which could adjust the gap in an outer cable, effectively shortening or lengthening the inner wire as conditions demanded. Like many good ideas it was remarkably simple.

The Motor Cycle's man Roy Morton also praised the general assembly of the machine which was built by Rogers from T45 chrome moly tubing and was regarded as a masterpiece of triangulation. With the engine being a common side to two triangles formed with the saddle tube and front down tube, top tube and lower tank tube. A triangle supports the steering head, another the rear wheel. Rogers is quoted as saying "the bike cannot be ridden by a lazy rider"; so stiff was the chassis that no power was wasted in frame flex. The chassis was copper-plated, lacquered and a real eye-catcher… just a shame there are no colour pictures.

DOUBLING UP

If one speedway engine is good then two must be better? So seemed the thinking when Australian sidecar speedway racers Jim Davies and Peter Speerin brought their double engine JAP outfit to the UK for some demos. Unlike solo speedway, the sidecar teams race clockwise and the outfits are pre-banked at 30 degrees. Speerin's outfit used two 500cc JAP engines – one mounted conventionally, the other mounted backwards and in its own subframe. The engines were connected by spur gearing between them and primary drive was by chain from the right-hand engine. The Davies outfit used a V-win JAP to get the 1000cc capacity for the bigger Australian tracks, it was felt perhaps 500cc outfits would be more suited to the UK race scene. Interestingly no mention was made of their passengers.

ABOVE: One engine not enough? Let's bung in another and see what happens.

RIGHT: Jack Young, a speedway champion of the 1950s.

SPEEDWAY SHUTDOWN – YES OR NO?

At the end of the 1950s a small feature in *The Motor Cycle* suggested speedway was on the way out. Tracks had declined, spectator support was decreasing and the spectacle with shale as opposed to cinder tracks was not as good. A plume of cinders from the rear wheel of four racers was a sight to behold claimed the cinder advocates; rubbish came the reply from the shale advocates. Both cinders and shale go 'dead' in their track feel, but shale can be rejuvenated easily. Both sides had their views, and it seemed to the writer that the track wasn't to blame. Most speedway races were won by the man first into the first corner and therefore little more than processions was the claim by those who said the sport had had it. Not so pointed out the fans as Barry Briggs proved in that year's world final by several times riding round those in front of him.

All sorts of reasons were offered as to why the original writer made his claim. Had, he suggested, team tactics spoiled the show? Should the bread and butter be rationed so more jam can be offered to

the winner thus encouraging racing rather than riding to finish to pick up the money? His final sentence was telling, "clearly the key is real, honest to goodness racing!" Talk about stirring up a hornet's nest.

The next issue but one of the publication had a reply from Cyril J Hart stating, just as forcefully, that speedway was going nowhere. He admitted speedway enthusiasts would be heartened to have had the original full page on their sport in the papers – a rare occurrence by the late 1950s – and added he realised the original piece had been the result of a great deal of thought.

On the subject of venues closing the later piece argued yes, that had been the case, but they were mainly the sorts of tracks opened because someone saw the opportunity to make a few quid then vanish rather than the enthusiastic operators who also saw the opportunity to make a few quid but wanted to carry on doing so. To do this the tracks had to operate as proper businesses, and those that did succeeded.

Track surface was not considered a huge influence on the spectator interest, what was influencing the decision to stay away was the lack of action on it.

No one will regularly pay to see a procession, spectators, many who weren't motorcyclists at all, will only pay to see action. Hart provided Swindon Robins as a prime example. A minor team until 1956 when they won the second division championship, they were promoted to division one and were then part of the group when it all became one big league. The side had a lacklustre start to the pre-season opener winning four of 10 races, but when the season started the Robins really flew and won their first eight matches – eventually going down to Birmingham well into the season. This was followed by a draw and another run of seven wins halted only by Belle Vue.

Crowd attendance at Swindon rose dramatically because there was something to watch and this competitive action, claimed Hart, was evidence that speedway still had a bright future ahead.

Two-valve Jawa

Massive engine plates hold the simple engine low down which is great for weight distribution and balance.

TOP LEFT: Clutch action is simple.

BOTTOM LEFT: Lever shrouds keep the dirt out of the clutch workings.

ABOVE: Developed from the ESO unit, Jawa was a tough engine which was easy to maintain and didn't cost as much as earlier units to keep it in tip-top condition.

From nowhere to everywhere in almost no time at all seemed to be the way Jawa grabbed the speedway scene by the twistgrip and took it to new levels. It helped of course that the importer/distributor could ride a bit and was a world champion, too. However, if the Jawa 890 hadn't been any good then even the talents of Barry Briggs would have been hard-pushed to promote it.

Luckily the 500cc motor was good and tough enough to handle the frenetic world of sideways racing. Whereas the previous backbone of the scene – JAP – was known to be fast it did take quite a bit of looking after and for the busy racer downtime meant no income. The Jawa wasn't faster than the JAP, but it was tougher which meant long spells between rebuilds and it was cheaper to maintain even when it did need the work.

Jawa sort of evolved from ESO, and arguably the bikes are badge-engineered ESOs because the company was absorbed into the Jawa corporation in 1964, but whatever it was called, a motorcycle was produced that could stay the distance. It was also produced by people who knew the scene and knew what was needed.

The motorcycle in our pictures was used by Eric Boocock in his British championship year, and is typical of what was being raced at the time. With a two-part, chromed oil-bearing frame, minimal suspension at

LEFT: Gearing might be changed any number of times during a meeting as track conditions improve and the racing is faster.

BELOW: Jawa's multi-plate clutch needs careful setting, but once set is a dependable unit… barring accidents of course.

BELOW: A small footrest is in place for the rider's left boot in those few seconds when it isn't on the track and supporting the bike.

Elastoplast rather than a grip or tape is the chosen cover for the twistgrip.

E Boocock

ABOVE: PAL's self-generating electronic magneto replaced the older mechanical Lucas racing ones of earlier years.

RIGHT: Legend…

State-of-the-art circa 1970s, the two-valve Jawa was quite capable of winning championships, as this one did with Eric Boocock on board, and also being the backbone of speedway.

the front and none at the rear the 890 was all about the race. The frame is from steel tubing and of open cradle type. Large engine plates mount the engine low down for an ideal weight distribution and give room for the countershaft gear box, obviously with no gears in as this is fixed speed stuff. The countershaft is there only because the clutch needs to hang on something.

The engine itself is an over-square all-alloy pushrod single, with two valves in the head. It's mounted vertically in the frame – the laydown era was still to come. Air-cooled, the 500cc motor uses a total-loss oil system in common with tradition. The oil pump feeding the lube to various parts of the engine is a double unit and one side pumps castor oil to the crankshaft, the other feeds it to the rocker mechanism in the head. The engine is a very clean design with everything covered to prevent muck and dirt getting into the workings.

A multi-plate clutch handles the job of getting the power to the wheel and, while not a complex item, it is a tough old thing given its working environment. The Jawa manual stresses the need for the clutch to lift cleanly and easily so the best possible start can be obtained.

Firing the methanol in the combustion chamber is by a PAL magneto mounted on the front of the engine and protected by a deflector plate. This ignition system is a step up from the old-fashioned type of magneto but operates on the same, self-generating principle. So, a good, tough motorcycle which only needed a good, tough rider to make best use of it… step up to the mark Mr Boocock.

WIMBLEDON STADIUM

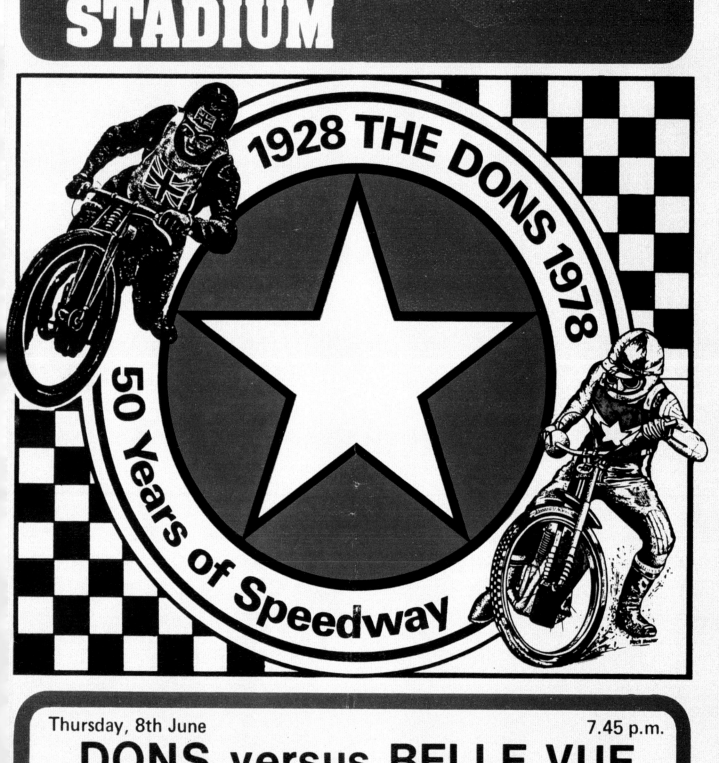

1928 THE DONS 1978

50 Years of Speedway

Thursday, 8th June   7.45 p.m.

DONS versus BELLE VUE
SPEEDWAY STAR KO CUP
Plus RICARD Second Half

Official Programme   20p

AHEAD OF HIS TIME

Though unusual when he was racing in the 1950s and 1960s, Peter Craven's riding style is distinctly modern with the bike much more upright and the rider hanging off the side. Not only did this style earn Craven two world championships and two British championships, but also the nickname The Wizard of Balance.

Like many of his contemporaries in the sport, young Craven came to the motorised version after racing the cycle version. A native of Liverpool, Peter tried out for the Liverpool Chads as soon as he turned 16, and he also raced for Fleetwood Flyers before earning a chance to race for the Belle Vue Aces in 1952. By 1953 he was a top-scoring team-member and even compulsory National Service didn't halt his ascendency.

He rode in his first world championship in 1954 – he'd qualify for 10 years in a row – and was champion in 1955. He would take the crown again in 1962, the same year he became British champ. He repeated the British championship in 1963 and seemed unstoppable until a freak accident to avoid a fallen rider at Edinburgh's Meadowbank Stadium cost the likeable lad his life.

Chapter 11

Hagon

Racer, record-breaker, manufacturer, supplier, inventor and sponsor are all descriptions which could be applied to Alf Hagon, whose business heads towards its 60th anniversary in 2018...

Is there a company out there that has done more for the grass track, speedway and sprint scene than the one which bears the name of Alf 'Mr grass track' Hagon? The team behind this publication doesn't believe so, and it's a company that's still going strong as it approaches its diamond anniversary; although these days it's under the day-to-day control of Alf's son Martin.

There have been changes, any company looking for longevity has to be flexible in its approach to business to be able to adapt to a market in a scene which can change rapidly. This was something Alf admitted in an interview with the press in 1978 where it was reckoned his success in sport was likely due to his versatility. It was a versatility he carried on into his business interests where his free-thinking approach to problem-solving led to many unique ways to advance the reliability and performance of the products used by sporting riders. During a recent visit to the current Hagon premises this versatility was still in evidence, so obviously the genes have been passed on.

The official beginning for Hagon Products was 1958, but such businesses rarely start out fully fledged and start dates tend to reflect when its founders went from 'doing stuff in a shed' to 'officially doing stuff in a shed'. Alf had been involved in motorcycle sport for quite a considerable number of years before 1958, usually running his own idea of what constituted the ideal machine. Naturally this ideal differed from the accepted norm, but what Alf was making and supplying was bringing him racing success, his ideas became the industry standard.

The story of that success had begun in the immediate post-Second World War period when a 15-year-old Alfred Joseph Hagon entered his first grass track race on a New Imperial which even then bore the signs of his attention. The competition bug had bitten and, as well as grass tracks, Alf took up scrambling on an ex-WD Matchless. When there weren't any scramble events to ride in he turned his hand to trials, too. A regular at Brands Hatch when it was a grass circuit pre-1950, he sorted out a four-valve 350cc Rudge road racer for the newly constructed Tarmac short circuit and he won the very first 350cc race held on that circuit in 1950. The interest in road racing didn't totally disappear either, and in the same year he started speedway as a Harringay team member he also rode a 500 Norton International in the Clubman's TT. Running eighth in the field at one point, he dropped to 29th when a stop to change a plug was forced on him. Despite all this it was obvious to the world that Hagon was inextricably linked with grass track and speedway and championships came his way with monotonous regularity; he also raced on the oval tracks for several teams such as Wimbledon, Leicester, Oxford and West Ham. His final speedway races came in 1965 when he retired from this hectic sport to concentrate on the shop he'd opened in East

Excellent preparation and neat touches marked Hagon machines out from the rest.

Not just solo stuff left the Hagon works.

Just supply your engine and go racing on the grass.

The suspension says it's for either grass, sand or long tracks.

A rubber-mounted footrest springs up in case of an accident, brake works the other way round.

Never a believer in resting on laurels, Alf Hagon realised the youth market needed a grass track bike so sorted a Honda Cub engine one.

BELOW: Dad and lad. A very young Martin Hagon poses apprehensively next to his dad Alf and the junior grass bike built for him.

ABOVE: Man and machine…

London in 1960. The lure of speed was too great though, and he had a dalliance with hill climbing and then went into sprinting where records were achieved with relative ease. This 'ease' masked a dedicated engineer quietly hard at work, and pretty soon the Hagon emporium was not only the place to go for your grass track and speedway requirements, but your sprint stuff too.

By 1970, when Alf decided his business needed the dedication he'd applied to his sporting achievements, he retired from sprinting with the world record for a standing-start kilometre to his name. Also by that time the Alf Hagon Products catalogue was 38 pages long and cost 25p. For the money the prospective grass track or speedway racer got access to a whole new world where performance was everything – and they could also purchase safe in the knowledge that everything in there was tested to the maximum by Alf himself, as well as a selection of the

Just the sort of machine future world champ Peter Collins went racing on at the start of his career.

For best results timing has to be spot on. The best way to achieve top dead-centre is with the cylinder head off; not always convenient, granted…

Alf was very hands-on in his approach to the manufacturing of bikes.

Design could be as intricate as this, or done on the back of a napkin in the local cafe…

current stars of the sideways world. Though almost synonymous with JAP power, the canny Hagon knew there were other suppliers in the wings and his frame kits for grass track, sand racing and speedway would accommodate Czech ESO – latterly Jawa – AMC and BSA singles, and it didn't stop there. Each discipline had a select number of parts, and while complete kits could be had, so could each and every part for servicing and damage replacement. Nothing was left to chance and each part listed had its own price. Alf's forethought made it easy for the racer to buy from him.

Sprinters or drag racers were not left out either and there were long, low frames, nosecones and engine tuning parts galore available. Technical tips were in there also, such as Alf's lore on making a JAP engine work properly – the bits needed in order to follow his suggestions were helpfully listed. So were tuning specs such as combustion chamber capacities and the compression ratio they equated to. For example if your 500cc cylinder head will hold 38cc of light oil as measured by a burette, then you can follow the mathematical formula to work out the compression ratio. Or you could look at the chart on page 11 to find out it is – 14.2:1 – then look down the page to match your gear ratios to track requirements. This was clearly a man who knew what was needed, and provided it.

Frame kits were designed around the popular engines of the time for grass track such as BSA's C15, B40 and Victor ranges, as well as the new two-strokes making an impact in the scene such as CZ and Husqvarna models. The enthusiast, who got as much pleasure from actually building their machine from scratch as they did riding, was not forgotten about and there were pages in the catalogue where tube, alloy sheet and plate could be bought in reasonable quantities. Once the bike was sorted then the rider could be taken care of with helmets, boots, leathers, overalls, steel shoes, gloves and goggles all listed making Hagon the true one-stop shop for the budding racer. Many of the parts and accessories were made or built in the Hagon

workshops where accuracy was the watchword – Alf himself acknowledged in *The Motor Cycle* feature that his attention to detail and professionalism brought repeat business to the company.

Not everything was designed in conventional ways, however. Take the monocoque sidecar chassis which Ton van Heugten used to win the European MX championship in the 1970s. Another example was Terry Rowing who was working at Hagon and made up his own sidecar frames in tubing – but they weren't holding

together. One lunchtime in the local cafe a thought occurred to Alf, a pen was acquired and the monococque concept was laid out on the back of a napkin. Four weeks later the outfit was ready and Terry won on it first time out. Dismissing the revolutionary concept as "nothing really new, just an extension of the engine plate idea…" was typical of the unassuming way Alf worked. Following on from this a deal with Vic Eastwood brought a solo version of the idea for the XT500 Yamaha single. This chassis incorporated fuel and oil tanks in the design which increased the stiffness of the whole chassis and saved a pound or three in weight.

Nor did the free thinking stop there, and with air shocks making their presence felt in the motocross world, Hagon came up with his own version for the grass track and long track scene. As with all of his concepts there were detailed instructions on how to service, maintain and adjust the shocks to suit the individual bike, owner and conditions. More remarkably there were other instructions and information on what would happen should the recommended minimum and maximum settings be exceeded, plus suggestions on how to deal with conditions where such extremes would be met.

These days Hagon still provides an extensive service to the speedway and grass track world – its involvement in the training facility at Lakeside Hammers is proof, should proof be needed – but also its shock absorber range is a major part of the company. When Girling sold off the rights to its rear dampers, Hagon was right there and the ones it makes are a development of those classic parts. The innovative thinking continues today as well, and the company is developing monoshocks for trials and road markets plus shock absorbers for all sorts of interesting and off-the-wall applications such as washing machines on oil rigs, electric mobility scooters, or how about seat dampers for semi-inflatable boats for the Danish navy? As Tony Hutcheson at Hagon said during research for this publication: "We'll do a shock absorber for any application that's required…"

SITTING IT OUT

Just because you're about to be the British League pairs champion, it doesn't mean it can't go wrong for you as Bruce Penhall finds out at Wimbledon in May 1978. Californian Penhall got his first taste of speedway when he was 16, and it didn't take long for him to become a regular in the USA championship; during 1976 he toured abroad. After making his mark in New Zealand and Australia he was offered a team place at Cradley Heath and it would be his home team for the next five years.

During that time Penhall won individual and team in both national and world championships before crowning his career with a world championship win in front of his home nation in the USA. With this championship Penhall announced his retirement from speedway and instead turned to acting; though with a motorcycle connection as he portrayed Officer Bruce Nelson in the TV series CHiPs. After speedway and acting, Bruce took up powerboat racing and lifted a world crown at that, too.

Totally wild

The speedway racer leads a pretty wild life, so where better to house a museum dedicated to the sport than a wildlife park...

ABOVE Grippy!

Motorcycle racing takes place under all sorts of conditions, but one of the most extreme has to be in the frozen winter-land of northern Europe when temperatures fall so low bikes have to be heated by blowers before they can be started. Ice racing is related to speedway, no sliding though as tyres are fitted with massive spikes which find grip… mostly.

This Jawa Ice Speedway bike was ridden by Zdenek Kudrna when he came 3rd in the World Ice Racing championship in 1979.

There are museums that contain soulless displays on their particular subject, with little thought for their presentation. Then there are museums with more enlightened curators and staff who go the extra mile to put some thought into their charges and display them in a setting which captures the past life of the exhibits. The National Speedway Museum is most certainly the latter. Housed in a building within Paradise Wildlife Park at Broxbourne in Hertfordshire even the colourful sign proclaiming the speedway museum's existence can't prepare you for what will assault your senses as you step through the door. Yes, there are bikes lined as you would expect, but there are also well-thought-out displays portraying the very essence of the sport and encouraging the visitor to think about how these machines earned their living, the riders who raced them, the engineers who developed them and the legions of fans who supported teams, cheered individuals and enjoyed the spectacle that is speedway.

PETER SAMPSON

After a race career which saw him compete at Rayleigh, Hackney, Swindon, Rye House and Newcastle, Peter Sampson never claimed to be a superstar but enjoyed his racing while investing in other businesses including a coach firm. An opportunity to purchase Broxbourne Zoo arose in the 1980s and Peter, with little knowledge of wild animals, took on the task of turning it into the success it is today. He maintained his interest in speedway and when the fledgling collection which would become the National Speedway Museum was looking for a home, Peter found space for it at Broxbourne. The collection is a major attraction for speedway enthusiasts and also a memory-jogger for non-motorcycling visitors who recall watching the Saturday afternoon races on the BBC and ITV sports programmes.

ABOVE: Old speedway racers never stop, they just have a season or two off.

ABOVE LEFT: One of the most successful early dirt track machines, Douglas's fore-and-aft twin. This is from the leg-trailing days at the birth of the sport in the UK.

LEFT: Can't fit everything in? Lift them up off the ground and double the space.

ABOVE: Thanks to an experiment by Barry Briggs, the speedway world embraced the 'laydown' concept of engine positioning, some say it spoiled the sport, some say it improved it.

ALAN SMITH

After finishing a meeting at King's Lynn in 1965, Alan Smith wheeled his bike into his shed likely intending to service it and sort it out for later. However, there it stayed until, several years after his death the 500cc JAP-powered machine was rediscovered. In tribute to the racer and to the rest of the unsung heroes who race week in, week out Alan's bike remains unrestored and just as found. We understand the display is a good recreation of how the bike was discovered. In the display are his helmet, steel shoe and the various spares, accessories and acquisitions of a racer's life.

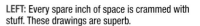

LEFT: Every spare inch of space is crammed with stuff. These drawings are superb.

BELOW: On the shelving behind the mannequin are patterns for casting engine parts such as crankcases, barrels and frame parts.

ABOVE: Many a top rider started their race career on the cycle speedways where skills were honed and fitness improved as pedal power was the way forward.

ABOVE: Wal Phillips was a racer, engineer, dealer and complete character. He developed the Wal Phillips Fuel Injector which was favoured by drag racers, and even fast road riders. Wal also produced his own engine which looks surprisingly modern for 1933.

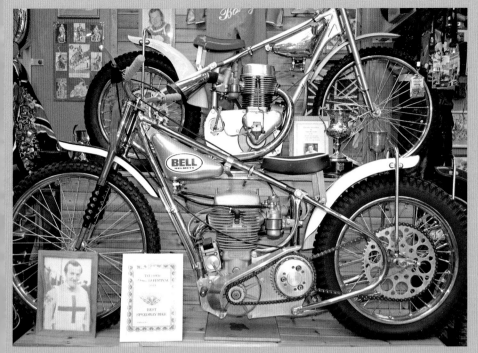

Possibly the winningest racer ever – six-time world champ Ivan Mauger loaned his Jawa for display.

Once Barry Briggs got to grips with the ESO marque – and after the company decided to change the title to Jawa after fuel giant ESSO had concerns about the similarities – Czech bikes were 'in.'

ABOVE: It isn't unusual to see brothers involved in motorcycle sport, and often one will cite the other as being responsible for his decision to have a go at racing, but the number of family pairings where both were successful is slightly fewer in number. The name 'Boocock' stirs the soul of speedway racers and polarises support, for one faction their 'Booey' is Nigel, resplendent in his blue leathers. Others lend their support to Nigel's younger brother Eric and their 'Booey' is the 'one' – noted for his well-turned-out machinery and dedication to the sport.

Sometimes the action in the pits of a meeting is as frantic as that on the track as riders struggle to sort out problems and faults in a desperate attempt to be ready for their next outing. A van is parked, its doors opened and tools strewn everywhere. The lucky ones have a mechanic, the rest just get on with it.

This Martin JAP was made by Victor Martin, a forward-thinking chap who not only made speedway machines, but was also co-promoter at West Ham.

THE WIZARD OF BALANCE

There are legends and there are LEGENDS… the latter is the late, great Peter Craven who raced for Belle Vue Aces. Twice world champion, the diminutive Craven developed his own style that relied on a delicate balancing technique and earned Craven the nickname The Wizard of Balance. In retrospect, he was the forerunner of the modern way. His Belle Vue career started in 1952 when he made his first appearance for the Aces, scoring two points. He was a regular, if less than auspicious, team member for the rest of the year but great things were to come. Elevated to permanent team-man, Craven scored 70 points out of 12 matches in 1953 despite having to complete National Service. Belle Vue veteran Jack Parker retired in 1954 and the promoter decided to build a team around Craven. It was to prove a good decision as Craven went on to win his first world championship in a nail-biting final against Barry Briggs.

Peter inspired many young lads to take up the sport, one such youngster who made a name for himself at Belle Vue was Peter Collins. Craven was lost to the speedway world in 1963 during a race at Edinburgh when a tragic set of circumstances ended with him colliding with the wooden fencing at the track.

CONTACT
The National Speedway Museum is at Paradise Wildlife Park in Hertfordshire
Web: pwpark.com
Tel: 01992 470490
Broxbourne, Hertfordshire, EN10 7QA

GOING INDOORS

"Browning stars in mini-speedway" screamed a headline in the sporting section of *The Motor Cycle*. It accompanied pictures of indoor speedway taking place at Whispering Wheels roller-rink in Wolverhampton with Arthur Browning and a selection of speedway racers, including Rob Homer, racing flimsy-looking speedway machines built from a BSA Bantam base. To the delight of the screaming fans, whose cheering drowned out the noise of the engines and the extractor units brought in to deal with exhaust fumes, Big Arthur forced the little Bantam around the 120-yard long track five times for a race best of 39.8 seconds. Talk about fast and furious!

In this photograph Arthur is about to pass Chris Harrison and would emerge top in the Best Pairs race with team-mate Andy Hunt after challengers Rob Homer and Howard Cole spun off into the safety fence. A full winter series of this light-hearted racing was promised.

Chapter 13

So you want to be a speedway racer?

You've seen the glamour on the telly, gone to the track, got caught up in the excitement and now there's the nagging thought eating away at you that you could be a speedway star. Tim Britton tells you what you need to know...

The Lakeside Hammers Saturday morning crowd.

During the 1930s speedway had gone from an oddball sport to a serious entertainment spectacle whose participants could and did earn considerable amounts of money. If the temptation was strong to try this sport for the ordinary working lad in the 30s then imagine the draw for servicemen looking for some excitement once the war was over. It was another Talmage feature, and he made no bones about it: if a rider had serious aspirations of succeeding in speedway then it would have to be their sole focus. Half-heartedness or divided loyalties would not bring the desired result and the prospective racer must be prepared for sacrifices, disappointment and heartaches in his chosen quest – and even then it might not bring rewards. In those dark days of June 1943 such a feature must have whetted the appetite of many a brave young lad, and while the author made the difficulties abundantly clear he also provided encouragement for those determined to try.

The first problem to overcome would be that of a motorcycle to ride. A speedway machine was by the 1940s so alien to a road machine that its only purpose was for racing on the cinders. A typical secondhand, but serviceable, machine was likely to cost £50 but that was only the start as leathers, boots, helmet, goggles, gloves and mask would have to be acquired. Imagine, too, that the prospective racer was based a long way from a track and couldn't realistically wheel the ▶

ABOVE LEFT: Learning to ride speedway in the old days meant a trip to a track where the sport could be tried.

ABOVE: At a track instruction would be given on starting...

LEFT: ...cornering at slow speed...

what to wear...

model there? He would have to find a way to get the machine there. Traditionally for the beginner this would be a sidecar with a flat platform – more cost – and this is all supposing that a track could be found in the first place.

Talmage admitted that the early part of his feature was designed to paint a potential speedway career at its worst, but suggested things might not be so difficult if two such prospective racers could team; they'd have to accept that one might end up being better than the other, but at least they both had a shot. Also, if the enthusiast wanted to try the sport and could raise the initial outlay only to find after a few laps the sport wasn't for them or the chosen mount not right, provided it hadn't suffered any damage it could be sold on at almost the purchase cost. For those still determined to try but not close to a track, it was suggested somewhere with loose gravel might be found which could give the feel of sliding a bike. Another suggestion was sand racing, as it was felt this could provide the necessary experience.

Assuming kit is bought and access to a

machine has been secured the apprenticeship could begin, claimed the writer. As the new rider is pushed away from the start line, the bike fires up and the full enormity of a 200lb – a tad under 91kg for those in new measures – machine with 40bhp and no brakes begins to dawn on the rider. The advice here was to take it slowly as to grab a handful of throttle would quickly end in disaster. No, the best way was to try a few laps, gradually increasing the speed until the only option to go faster is to slide. Talmage stated the change from riding round the corners to actually sliding had to be a conscious and committed decision and wasn't something to be tackled half-heartedly. The motorcycle had to be banked over and going fast enough for something to happen – a bit of a vague statement, true, but qualified by the writer saying he could only describe certain conditions and leave it up to the individual to interpret.

It has to be understood at this time there would have been readers whose only exposure to the sport would be the descriptive writing and accompanying images in the magazine

ABOVE: …cornering at high speed…

LEFT: …and what to carry in the support truck.

magazine features; there were no TV sports programmes or internet with film clips to explain things. Talmage likened the cornering experience to that of a road machine when, banked into the bend, the front wheel had a tendency to turn inwards – this was exactly what a speedway machine wanted to do unless it was checked by opening the throttle to encourage the rear wheel to spin. This, our man said, would pick the wheel up and restore control to the rider who would then turn the bars so the wheel would be pointing in the opposite way to the corner.

As a motorcycle slides on dirt there was apparently a tendency for a ridge of dirt to build up and the spinning rear wheel clears this allowing the bike and rider to progress round the corner as fast as possible. Talmage felt he might be stating the obvious by saying the more the throttle was opened the more the rear wheel slid out and the more lock on the bars was needed to sort this out. It was important though not to open the throttle too viciously as the back wheel would step right out and the bike go into a flat spin thus putting the rider in a heap. This in itself wasn't deemed a necessarily bad thing as the rider would learn from it and soon realise perhaps he'd been a tad harsh on the throttle and hadn't counteracted enough with the bars. This brought out two golden rules for successfully negotiating a speedway track – they being (number one) never be ham-handed with the twistgrip; and (number two) always open the throttle more if difficulties arise on a turn.

To jump forward 40 and 70 years, briefly,

those two rules were essentially what I was told in both my attempts at speedway and I found out the hard way what happens if the throttle is closed in a bend; the rider is pitched over the top of the bike and ends in a heap, usually in pain.

Anyway, back to story, once the novice has grasped this peculiar method of riding a motorcycle his next step would be to try it with three other riders on the track and his learning could really begin. The newcomer was still a long way from being able to make this sport pay, but would still have the expenses of running and maintaining his machine, suffering the setbacks and heartaches of any professional sport. It was at this point, Talmage mused, that many novices feel they are getting nowhere and chuck the whole lot in. However, the man that doesn't – the one who sticks at it and overcomes adversity – may well find himself achieving success in small-time races, picking up some prize money here and there and, more importantly, this is where he will be noticed by promoters. Once that has happened and some form of contract signed – 'Approved Form of Speedway Rider's Agreement for Service' was the term used in those far-off days – the bottom rung of the ladder has been reached.

Once this momentous day

has arrived Talmage suggested the novice could be better served going to a second division team – while starting and prize money was a lot less than a first division team he was likely to get more regular rides and thus increase his earning potential. The lad who went to a first division team might have the kudos of being there, but may spend a lot of time sitting in the pits desperate for a ride.

Also, in the second division the novice will learn team tactics, when to ride flat out, when to ride cautiously and become a proper team man. With this experience being gained the rider is no longer a novice and is actually heading up the ladder until that almost inevitable stage is reached when good riders hover a rung or two from the top for a season or two; yes they're good but they're not aces just yet. It's often unfathomable why a rider can't make the next step up; this is tried, that is tried until, perhaps, a chance remark by a top-line mechanic will suggest an alteration to a machine which propels the rider upwards. Or it may well be pure chance with the top man in the team crocked, the match is at a critical stage and it is the chance the newcomer has been waiting for. He is called to the start, the crowd are chanting his name, the boost is tremendous and almost overwhelming but his apprenticeship has been good, he's paid attention on his way up, despite the elation he has an ice-cool spot in his brain working out what needs to be done… a brief moment of time flashes past, mere seconds really, his hard-learned tactics are brought into play, his skills honed on tracks around the country are so natural he doesn't need to think about them… he can and will win… and he does to the roar of the crowd… the novice who tentatively slid his first motorcycle several seasons ago is now an overnight star.

THE AFTERMATH

With stardom achieved the rider is now in demand and his earnings are increasing, he is popular, he makes personal appearances and now the road ahead has two directions. Down one road there are wild parties – usually at the new superstar's expense – days spent on the golf course, new hobbies such as flying and expensive sports cars with no room for bikes or mechanics who still have to travel to meets which all costs money. It's okay though because the star is earning well… until he isn't. Almost as quickly as he burst on to the scene he's now last week's news, he's back in second division scratching for prize money as he's not thought about any other way of earning a living. The second road is for more of, a thinker, shall we say; it's taken

Most importantly though was track time, nothing beats track time.

£20 as instructed. The £20, a fair slice of my 1980 wage, was to hire a bike, leathers and steel shoe – and I would pay for fuel and oil as I used them. What awaited me was a two-valve Jawa, some button-up leathers (I'm a bit bigger than the usual speedway rider and this old pair of leathers was all that would fit me). I seem to recall there was a chat about previous experience, some questions to find out what we novices were expecting from the day, then we were out on the track.

Rather like Talmage's description of what happens on a speedway machine, the only proper way to find out was to try. After several laps riding round the track I was waved in and I was instructed to, and I quote: "Stop being a trials rider!" It seems the instructors on the day could generally tell what experience a rider had or what sport they'd competed in as grass track racers cornered one way, road riders another, MXers different again and trials riders try to ride round feet-up; the concept of foot forward, weight off the back wheel and opening the throttle was totally alien to me and I kept shutting the throttle instead of opening it. Exactly as Talmage had suggested, by doing this I was pitched over the top to land in a heap. Eventually it sunk in what was actually required, or maybe I just got lucky and happened to do everything right and I did manage to actually slide the back round. Unfortunately I carried on sliding around and ended in a heap again, but at least I'd not gone over the top this time. As shown by the complete lack of my name anywhere in the speedway annals

him a long time to become an overnight star, he also realises the punishing schedule of racing five nights a week in the season will take its toll on him and his machines. This, he decides, is a full-time job with little room for the glamour, it is also a full-time job which has a very short life span at the very top. He realises his annual earnings are limited to a six-month period when the season is in full swing, perhaps over winter a job is taken to provide living expenses so the prize money can be saved – or maybe he'll winter in Australia and race there. His top-flight stardom is maybe three seasons; there will be a few seasons either side of that where he is a top racer and earning well so able to put his earnings to use for that inevitable day when he realises he is no longer the star, but unlike the party animal he is still bankable; and if he's been smart enough his name means something and he is able to run a business where that name increases the earning potential. Perhaps he could become a dealer or even a speedway promoter, in short his determination which took him from tentative novice to superstar is still bringing its rewards and he nods appreciatively at the memory of that long ago feature which set him on that path.

THAT WAS THEN...

The next part of this story is not quite now, but it's a lot closer to now than the 1940s. It starts with an admission: I'm a trials rider... there it's out! But in the local club which my father and uncle had been members of during their competition days was a speedway rider – yes he was a trials rider, too, and sickeningly good at both disciplines. Anyhow this speedway rider, Dave Younghusband, was just coming to the end of his top-level professional days and becoming more involved in managing teams. So, one day as a lad, I asked him the completely naïve question: how do you become a speedway racer? "Get a bike, come down to Brough Park and have some second half rides..." came the reply. Oh. Er. But if I wanted to try it first? "There's a training track at Felton in Northumberland, give the lad a call and go up," he said then snicked his Bultaco into gear and waltzed feet-up through a section which had defeated the entire field so far.

Call the lad I did and, more in the spirit of wanting to try than with any great aims to be a professional speedway racer, I headed for this track with my crash helmet, boots and

ABOVE: Just lapping on the bike builds confidence.

BELOW: The important steel shoe has changed little over the years.

ABOVE: Leathers or protective kit has changed a bit.

ABOVE: At the track there would be regulars who would offer tips as they watched you circulate.

BELOW: Almost at the point of sliding.

I didn't go on to have a glittering career, but I'd tried it and was happy with that.

FAST FORWARD TO NOW...

"When you coming down to the speedway academy then, Tim?" said Hagon's Tony Hutcheson during a phone chat about suspension units. "Hmm, not sure, Tony," was my reply. "I tried speedway years ago and wasn't very good at it." "Neither am I," he replied, "but I'm there on a Saturday morning going round with all the gear and no idea." So, the day after meeting up with Colin Knight and photographing his collection of classic speedway machines at Hagon's premises, I'm on the way to the Lakeside Hammers and Hagon Shocks' Speedway Academy at Arena Essex for my second go at speedway in 40 years.

Things have moved on a bit since my first attempt – specifically in the sport and in more of a general context. Laydown bikes are the thing these days and at the academy smaller bikes are in. The track is less than 100 metres so, unless you're a very good rider a full size 500 would be near enough impossible to get round. What Hagon have is 140cc four-strokes with full-sized wheels which give the

BELOW: More starting practice.

flavour of what speedway is all about.

Something else which has changed in recent years is the use of air cushions on the bends. Exactly as the name implies, these are cushions filled with air and hitting one is a lot less nasty than whapping into the solid board fence would be. Yes, safety is the key word here and the experience is all the better for it too.

Speaking with Gerald Richter, who seems to hold the whole thing together, about the academy and his role in it he revealed there were other training centres around the country but this one was the only one where the whole package could be arranged. That package is bike, clothing, safety equipment, fuel and oil, plus track time all in the hire charge. There are several scales of charge depending on age and whether or not you're bringing your own gear, so for the latest scoop go to the Lakeside Hammers website and see what's what. Gerald continued by telling me the whole idea of the academy is to encourage new blood into racing, something it's been very successful at. "At the Rye House youth championships there were seven riders from this school in the racing," he explained. Beginners attending this school are taught the right way to ride competitively and safely which makes them better riders.

There are three styles of bike available for hire at the track: two 140cc models with Chinese Stomp engines in, and one 250cc version which has a Jawa motor. For the 140cc bikes there's a kids' version with small wheels and an adult version with full-size wheels – and don't go getting the idea these 140s are slow and pedestrian, they go plenty fast enough when wound on and are more than capable of power-sliding. On the day that I turned up there were one or two people on

ABOVE: Tips will be available on kit preparation, too.

BELOW: Everything is on the right, so if there's a spill then less damage occurs.

The thrill of the race.

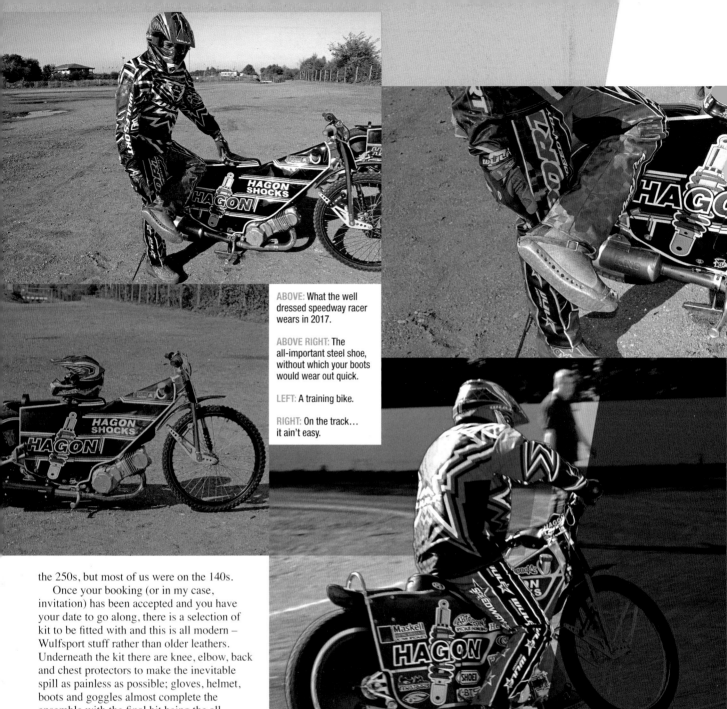

ABOVE: What the well dressed speedway racer wears in 2017.

ABOVE RIGHT: The all-important steel shoe, without which your boots would wear out quick.

LEFT: A training bike.

RIGHT: On the track… it ain't easy.

the 250s, but most of us were on the 140s.

Once your booking (or in my case, invitation) has been accepted and you have your date to go along, there is a selection of kit to be fitted with and this is all modern – Wulfsport stuff rather than older leathers. Underneath the kit there are knee, elbow, back and chest protectors to make the inevitable spill as painless as possible; gloves, helmet, boots and goggles almost complete the ensemble with the final bit being the all-important steel shoe. This allows the rider to take the weight of the bike on his or her (there's no ban on ladies now) left foot and still slide the bike like it should be done. Before we took to the track there was a riders' meet where questions were answered, and for the organiser to be sure we knew the sequence of flags, although thankfully only two were needed – the black and yellow 'last lap' and the chequered 'finish' ones.

With no gears to worry about and a kill switch on a lanyard attached to the rider's right wrist to stop the motor, it was clutch in and a volunteer pushed each rider away. The first few laps were to familiarise myself with the machine, just as well really as for some reason I had a problem finding the footrest at first. Once that little problem was sorted there was track positioning to cope with which involved cones being placed at various points to create a different route round the 96m oval. In our group there were a number of different abilities and it is to the credit of Gerald and his team that, broadly speaking, abilities were matched for each track session so we slower ones weren't intimidated by the faster racers. After each session on the track the instructors would

have a word and offer advice to "get forward on the bike" or "open the throttle sooner" and by the end of the day everyone had progressed to a greater or lesser degree, but I still realised by the end that this speedway lark is just going to have to manage without my less-than-glittering skills on the track.

ONWARDS AND UPWARDS

So, you've done the training bit, you've got handy on the small bikes, progressed to the 250s and made the jump to 500s. The next step is to get noticed as an up-and-coming rider – a hard slog of going to tracks all over the country trying to get promoters to notice you. Once you're good enough for your talents to be scouted, then a club may well approach you and offer you rides at their home facility. The big question then comes; can a living be made from sliding a motorcycle around a dirt track? The answer is yes, but for every superstar

there are lots more team members doing okay, treating it like a job where you turn up, do your best and earn your crust.

Lakeside Hammers
The Hagon Shocks
Speedway Academy
Arena Essex Raceway
A1306 Arterial Rd
Purfleet
Essex
RM19 1AE
Web: lakesidehammers.co.uk
Tel: 01708 863443

For academy booking contact
Gerald Richter
Tel: 07973 839 056
Email: spdwy@hotmail.co.uk